The **Advanced Cyclist's** Training Manual

A&C Black · London

Luke Edwardes-Evans

The **Advanced Cyclist's** Training Manual

FITNESS AND SKILLS FOR EVERY RIDER

Note

Whilst every effort has been made to ensure that the content of this book is as technically accurate and as sound as possible, neither the author nor the publishers can accept responsibility for any injury or loss sustained as a result of the use of this material.

Published in 2010 by A&C Black Publishers Ltd
36 Soho Square, London W1D 3QY
www.acblack.com

Copyright © 2010 Luke Edwardes-Evans

ISBN 978 1 4081 0870 3

A CIP catalogue record for this book is available from the British Library.

Acknowledgements
Cover photograph © Gerard Brown
Inside photographs © Gerard Brown, except pp87-88 © Grant Pritchard
Illustrations by Jeff Edwards pp28, 31, 38; Mark Silver p138
Designed by Lilla Nwenu-Msimang
Commissioned by Charlotte Croft
Edited by Kate Turvey

This book is produced usin   aged,
sustainable forests. It is r   ; and
manufacturing processes co   untry
of origin.

Typeset in 9pt MetaPlus Nor   erby

Printed and bound in China

Contents

Acknowledgements

Many thanks to Gerard Brown for all the photography, both current and back catalogue, his unflappable good humour and belief in the project; Chris Sidwells for additional copy, coaching expertise and invaluable access to and knowledge of cycle racing; John Herety, the riders and support staff of team Rapha-Condor for their patience and time at their annual training camp; Phil Cavell at CycleFit for bike set-up; Sean Yates for the foreword; Charlotte Croft for making it happen and Kate Turvey for pulling it all together.

Foreword

When I look back at my 15-year career as a professional cyclist it gives me great pride to think of the thousands of miles I raced in countless countries across the globe. In that time I rode 12 Tours de France and had the ultimate privilege of wearing the yellow jersey for a day during the 1994 Tour.

The mountains of the Tour de France were never my favourite place to race a bicycle, but I loved to ride through the great mountain ranges of Europe and am still thrilled to see those legendary mountain passes over which I suffered so much! These days I usually see them from the driving seat of my Sky team car as I direct and encourage young professionals going through the same experiences that I did all those years ago.

I also loved racing on the flat, cobbled roads of northern Europe and my fifth place in the Paris-Roubaix classic and other top finishes in the 'Queen of the Classics' in the 1990s were the result of countless hours of hard training and meticulous planning.

Riding at the highest level I had to take my training as seriously as any professional sportsperson, not just on the road but also in terms of recovery, diet and planning. You may not have the time to adopt the lifestyle of a professional, but whatever your level the principles of training remain the same.

In this book the authors have stressed the importance of setting goals, and creating training plans to work through and beyond each one. Cycling is a tough, unforgiving sport. If you want to achieve something in cycling there are no shortcuts – hard work and determination will pull you through, but you also need to know when to back off, rest and recover.

It's easy to get sucked into the science of training and these days there are numerous ways to monitor and track your progress through testing, heart rate and power. These tools are invaluable and I have always found a regular test is a great indicator of my current level of fitness. You can read about various ways to monitor your level in this book.

I had a reputation as a bit of a hard man when I was a professional rider – I might even have put the wind up Lance Armstrong now and again when he came under my wing as a neo-pro on the Motorola team way back when! These days, working as a directeur sportif with professionals half my age, I try to pass on my knowledge of how to survive as a pro, but I also try to show how much I love cycling and what cycling has given me as a person. Fundamentally that is why I am still in this great sport – because I have a passion for it that life's inevitable lows cannot dim. Carry that passion for cycling inside you and you will achieve your cycling goals.

Sean Yates

Introduction

Welcome to *The Advanced Cyclist's Training Manual*

Whatever your particular interest in the many different disciplines, *The Advanced Cyclist's Training Manual* is packed with advice, training plans and encouragement to help you become a fitter, faster, safer and healthier rider.

Following on from *The Cyclist's Training Manual*, this advanced edition addresses the same wide cycling base, but focuses more intently on the core functions of training, bike set-up, technique and health. If you are a more experienced rider, this book aims to inform and inspire you to take your cycling to new levels of achievement.

We have concentrated on the competitive cyclist, without assuming you're a regular weekend racer. Today's serious riders are motivated by a far wider range of cycling challenges than existed 25 years ago, when racing on the road was pretty much the only choice.

The boom in cyclo-sportives has generated massive interest from a new breed of cyclist willing to train to high levels and ride as hard and long as a traditional 'racer'. For some, the annual goal of a gold medal ride in one of the classic European sportives is motivation enough to follow a serious training programme. Racing has also become a more accessible sport, with events on- and off-road for every level of ability. *The Advanced Cyclist's Training Manual* will get you and your bike into shape and on the start line in the best possible shape.

What's in *The Advanced Cyclist's Training Manual*?

The cycling year unfolds naturally from the end of the previous session, into winter training, spring speed, summer racing and autumn challenges. In this book we have followed the rhythm of the cycling year, starting with self-assessments and planning, and progressing through the seasons as the year rolls on. Sections on machine set-up and technique come early on when there is time in the off-season to hone and adjust.

Professional and elite riders talk about their own training and racing experiences in every chapter, giving an insight into the real lives of top cyclists. I hope you find their hard won advice invaluable and inspiring.

- *Chapter 1: You and your cycling* – We start with pre-season self assessment and analyse your lifestyle, work and family commitments. This leads on to goal setting and your annual plan. Testing on the bike to find your current level is also important.

- *Chapter 2: The language of fitness* – This chapter deals with understanding how the processes of training work including muscle types, genetics and training, heart rate, VO_2 max, and lactate myths. We also cover power and power-weight.

- *Chapter 3: Bike fitting* – A vital chapter on the essential checks and adjustments needed to optimise power, comfort and aerodynamics. We cover saddle height, upper body position, 'in the cockpit', crank length and Q-factor, and shoe plate adjustment. Time trial riding position and aerodynamic equipment is also discussed.

- *Chapter 4: Riding technique* – This chapter covers how to hone your riding skills for faster safe progress, cornering technique and corner types, thinking ahead, braking, riding in the wet, what to do when it goes wrong and cadence.

- *Chapter 5: Endurance* – We focus on building an endurance base after the autumn break, the five training zones, endurance training plans through the winter months, and using your ride to work to gain valuable endurance miles.

- *Chapter 6: Love winter!* – This chapter includes ideas on finding alternatives to cycling during the winter months, including gym training sessions, running, skiing and skating. Also included are weight training techniques and exercises, cyclo-cross and mountain biking, motor pace training and winter track riding and racing.

- *Chapter 7: Fast fuel* – Here we cover everyday eating plans and on the bike re-fuelling, carbohydrate and glycaemic index, good fats and bad fats, protein, alcohol, water and drinking on the bike, portion control, and supplements.

- *Chapter 8: From endurance to power* – Adding speed after the winter endurance phase is the focus of this chapter, as well as cyclo-cross and mountain bike workouts and technique. We discuss riding singlespeed or fixed wheel, turbo training sessions, riding rollers and threshold intervals.

- *Chapter 9: Peaking for summer* – This chapter discusses how to settle into training and competition when the season begins. We also cover periodisation in the short and longer term, training plans for summer riding and peak form.

- *Chapter 10: All out!* – We cover the big day, how to tackle a race or challenge event, as well as riding in a group, team time trialling technique, how to win a road race, coping with fast starts, road sprinting tips and packing your race bike and kit.

- *Chapter 11: Injury and overtraining* – We show you how to cope with the lows of cycling and crash injuries including cuts, breaks and head injuries, injuries to knees, back and contact points. Also covered is overtraining – how to spot it and avoid it, and recovering from serious overtraining.

- *Chapter 12: So much to do...* The final chapter includes races and challenges to inspire and enjoy: road racing, time trials, cross-country, cyclo-cross, track, challenge events, cyclo-sportive, touring and training camps.

You and your cycling

Would you be reading this book if you were not already nuts about cycling, eager to improve and possibly looking for some advice on cycling events to inspire and challenge you? This is not a book for beginners – we're assuming you have been riding for at least a year or so and have a pretty shrewd idea of your favourite type of cycling, some targets to aim for and the level of fitness you need to acquire in order to achieve your goals.

Just a mouse click away there is a never-ending output of training theory and advice on the internet but, while much of it is genuinely interesting and informative, it rarely addresses the individual with his or her own lifestyle, work, family or physical issues. To make the most of your training, the first thing you need to do is make an honest, if not brutally frank, assessment of your own personal circumstances, taking a cold hard look at your current physical condition, your health and weight, and how much time you can realistically devote to attaining your goals.

Cyclists are high achievers, they relish a challenge and are not afraid of hard work. Sound familiar? That's something to be proud of, but it also pays to be realistic when it comes to planning your cycling year. A professional cyclist can spend between 15 and 30 hours a week on the bike. That might not sound much – it's less than one full day per week – but if you break it down into a daily ride it's at least two hours every day, and often very much more.

If you are lucky enough to be able to incorporate your training into your daily commute, piling up professional quantities of training is achievable. But what full-time riders have lots of – and you most likely do not – is time to rest. Without that vital aspect to your training, you will soon find yourself overwhelmed by fatigue, which can lead to illness, injury and stress. Be realistic about the training you can do, and create a plan which dovetails most neatly into your busy life, and you will have made a crucial first step on the road to a long and successful cycling career.

External factors thus accounted for, pre-season job number two is to make a physical self-assessment. This is the bit where you sit down with a piece of paper, or page one of your training diary, and make notes regarding your current state of fitness, your body shape, your strengths and weaknesses on the bike and your overall state of health. It's also the time to identify some key targets in the coming 12 months. It's no good being anything other than searingly honest with yourself, as what you conclude from the results of this self-assessment will determine how you structure the season, your preferred training sessions, and the probability of achieving goals along the way.

A cup of tea, a pencil, paper and a ruler

It's time to get real about you, your cycling and your life around cycling. After a half-hour or so you should be looking at a page divided into three parts, with questions answered in each section. The three areas you need to address are:

- My cycling goals
- My lifestyle
- Me!

This is not necessarily a solo project as parts one and two are directly related to your own personal circumstances, which could include being a student living at home, single with a part-time job, a parent of a young family, or retired on a pension.

If you only have to answer to yourself, lucky you! If you have to take into account the needs of others, then it might be wise at this point to discuss your cycling hopes and dreams, and how they fit in, with loved ones, friends and colleagues. Achieving a consensus on these weighty matters will be appreciated by other halves and reduce your guilt pangs every time you clip-clop out the back door. Cycling is a time-consuming sport and you need to be a little bit stubborn and selfish to follow a season-long programme. Don't make it harder for yourself or those close to you by presenting your cycling manifesto as an ultimatum.

My cycling goals

Blue-sky thinking here; if you want to win a race in the next six months that's great, put it down. If you want to knock ten minutes off your favourite long distance sportive, that's good too. But your goal could be to climb your local hill faster than last year, on your own, with no cheering crowds, purely for your own satisfaction. Stick it down, it's right up there with the others. Or perhaps you want to lose a stone in weight and ride nonstop for 60 miles. Make sure your goals are personal, measurable and something you can put a time on by saying 'I want to achieve such and such by this time'.

Don't base your goals on things or people which can change or let you down. Vowing to beat your mate in a club time trial is not a good idea as you have no control over how well or badly they could be going a few months down the road. However, achieving a certain time in that time trial is something you do have control over, as you can train in a way that systematically increases the average speed at which you ride over a set distance. Now, that time might also be quick enough to beat your mate. Get the picture?

Answer the following questions about your cycling goals:

- What are my three goals in the next six months?
- What are my five goals in the next twelve months?
- What is my goal for the next two years?
- What is my all-time cycling goal?

My lifestyle

Take a metaphorical step back and look at your life as a whole. This part is not just about you, it's about you and your job, your studies and your free time. Just as importantly it's about your family, friends and colleagues.

The point of this is a reminder that there are things going on outside of your obsession with the bike that you might like to acknowledge in writing. Things that, when you see them in black and white before you, are in fact very important to your wellbeing, heart and soul. These are the aspects of your life that you need to recognise, nurture and protect. Cycling need not be a corrosive influence: on the contrary, be the master of your sport and there's no reason why it should not enhance the quality of your life and the lives of those around you.

The questions below are a guideline and at this point it might be helpful to involve your partner or best buddy in the planning process. They can give you feedback on how they feel about your cycling and whether you are taking yourself rather too seriously over it.

Answer the following questions about your life situation:

- Who are the loved ones/friends I want to spend time with?
- What are my work commitments?
- Are my work commitments the same each week?
- How much time can I devote to training each week?
- What am I like when I cycle a lot?
- What am I like when I cycle very little?
- What puts me off riding my bike?
- Am I a cycling bore or does cycling make me more interesting?
- Do I get the cycle–life balance right?

Me!

Grab a clean sheet of paper for part three of your pre-season self-assessment and record your answers to the items in the table opposite. It's unlikely you will have all the answers in one sitting and you may even need to line up some on-bike tests to complete every question. If you have been riding seriously for any length of time, chances are that you will have already acquired a heart rate monitor, an indoor turbo trainer with a computer readout or a power measuring crank. Even if you haven't, a basic cycle computer or even a stopwatch can be used to make a start on gathering baseline data which you will find invaluable once the real riding begins.

MEASURING POWER

Power, measured in watts, can be displayed and stored by on-bike power metering systems, the most widely known being the German SRM system. Many professional riders use chainsets modified to take the SRM strain gauge, which measures pedalling forces and transmits the data to a handlebar-mounted display unit. Costing as much as a top end racing bike, the SRM system is a serious commitment, but an invaluable aid to training. Another popular system is the PowerTap meter which measures strain through a custom-made rear hub. Power is also displayed and stored by a bar-mounted computer. A more affordable alternative to bike-mounted power meters is a turbo trainer with a power output display. These top-end indoor trainers may not measure power with the same accuracy as an SRM, but they can be a valuable indicator of levels of effort and training progress.

TABLE 1.1: PERSONAL DETAILS

Height

Weight over last 12 months

Body mass index (BMI)

Resting heart rate

Maximum power output

Personal best times in racing or training

Ramp test results

Best results or performances (last year and personal bests)

Number of years cycling

Current racing category

Current time devoted to training each week

Strengths

Weaknesses

Opportunities

Threats

KNOW YOUR BMI

Your BMI figure is an indication of your bodyweight compared to your height. There are numerous websites which will automatically calculate your BMI if you input your age, height and weight. A figure between 18.5 and 25 is considered ideal, with below 18.5 considered underweight and over 25 overweight.

KNOW YOUR RESTING HEART RATE

This test is best done within 10 minutes of waking in the morning. Get up, make a cup of tea and go back to bed, sitting up and awake. After a few minutes of sitting still take your resting heart rate, either from the reading on your heart rate monitor, or by counting the pulse in your wrist over 60 seconds. Doing this a few times a week will give you an accurate indication of your resting heart rate.

The last four items on the list in table 1.1 are also known as SWOT analysis (strengths, weaknesses, opportunities, threats). SWOT is a commonly used abbreviation in business which gets down to the core facets of a proposition or an opportunity. This analysis can work for you, but you need to be honest with yourself.

Under strengths you should find it relatively easy to pinpoint which aspects of cycling you excel at. Most likely they will be things like climbing, sprinting, time trialling, bike handling, endurance or tactics. They could also be your ability to train hard, shrug off bad weather, stay healthy throughout the year, achieve your racing weight, or maintain focus or love of winning.

Weaknesses could be the opposite of any of the strengths, but they could also include parts of them that you feel you are weak at, such as bunch riding, riding in the heat, susceptibility to colds, inability to build on success, or an addiction to cakes and biscuits!

Listing your riding opportunities is the chance for you to list the races, events and challenges that you already take part in, but it's also an opportunity for you to think outside the box and add to the list of cycling activities that you may not have experienced before, but have always fancied doing. Be bold but realistic – if you want to ride a mountain bike race in the next 12 months it would be wise to start with a local one before sending your entry off to the Crocodile Trophy in the Australian Outback.

You can test yourself on a turbo trainer.

Opportunities should also include the different environments in which you can train, like a gym at work, nice roads near your home or experienced, friendly cyclists to ride with.

Threats cover the logistical hurdles that you'll need to clear in order to achieve your cycling goals. Can you afford to pay for your bikes and kit, travel to events, entries and licences? Take into account the hours that you work and figure out roughly how much you will need to budget for.

Test yourself

Testing is the only way to know how well you are going from a completely objective standpoint. Finding ways to test yourself throughout your cycling career is essential to your self-knowledge as a rider, and the feedback and figures from testing can confirm that you are doing everything right, or else flag up issues that you need to address.

Racing cyclists test themselves each time they pin on a number, and their results are an ongoing indicator of form and training. Even so, there are many 'known unknowns' in racing that make it a far from ideal measure of your base condition. An objective test at least once every three months is worth fitting into the busiest racing schedule, and should be carried out more often if you do not race very much, maybe as often as every month to six weeks.

You can test yourself with a basic stopwatch and a stretch of road, a hill or a circuit. At the other end of the scale you could have everything monitored and measured, from power to lactate acid levels and VO_2max, in a sports laboratory. In between are the most common methods to determine your fitness level – using a turbo trainer with a heart rate monitor or a power measuring system.

Don't be deterred if all you have is a local stretch of road and a stopwatch, as in many ways this is as close as you can get to the real world conditions that you are training for. As long as the weather conditions are relatively benign, the test figures along this stretch of road will, if anything, be more relevant than those obtained in the uninspiring surroundings of a static bike in a lab or even on a turbo trainer in your shed. No looking at the scenery though – unless you go flat out every time, the figures will be meaningless.

Five-mile time trial
Find a safe stretch of road about 15 minutes away from your house. Think about your local area and identify an out-and-back course or short circuit with safe left-hand turns only. It needs to be about five miles in length with start and finish points, such as signposts, clearly identifiable by you. Above all make sure it's on safe roads, preferably well surfaced with predictable traffic and minimum distractions. Flat or rolling is the best terrain: forget off-road, as a spell of rain could double your time.

Use the same bike each time you do a test, pump up your tyres to the same pressure, and ideally carry the tests out at the same time of day and in a rested condition, with no hard training during the 48 hours preceding the test. You need to be well hydrated and carry a weak-mix energy drink that you can sip right up to the start. Make sure that your last meal is fully digested. The 'same bike, fully rested' rule should apply to any test you do.

Use the ride to the start of the course as your warm-up, throwing in a couple of one-minute efforts to 'open up' the legs. Roll up to the start and begin timing or recording the session on your stopwatch, heart rate monitor or power meter. Get up to speed smoothly, at a fast cadence around 90rpm. Ride the course as fast as you can without blowing up. It's not a sprint and will need lots of concentration and pace control. You should cross the finish line with just enough energy left to stop the watch at your chosen place.

Warm down on the ride home, spinning a low gear to recover. Back home, note down the following in your training diary:

- Conditions of the test (time of day, weather, temperature)
- Test time
- Average heart rate
- Maximum heart rate
- Average power
- Maximum power
- Perceived effort (*see* page 000)
- Body weight
- Any additional factors (e.g. bike used, clothing)

A five-mile time trial should take between 10 (30mph average speed) and 15 minutes (20mph average speed) and is the shortest distance for this type of test. You could ride up to 30 minutes on a similar course or, if you have a steady climb in your area that takes 10 to 20 minutes to ascend, time yourself from the bottom to the top.

VAM

Climbing tests are favoured by many professional riders as they guarantee a high level of effort and are also a great indicator of climbing power and strength to weight ratios. These tests also give them a figure known as VAM, or Velocity Ascended in Metres per hour. This is a vertical figure given in metres (from about 1,000 to 1,800 for Tour de France riders) which can be compared to climbing performances across a range of hills of different lengths and gradients. It's a good indicator of climbing power and due to the slower speeds on a climb, is much less affected by the effects of wind resistance on a rider on the flat. As the times taken to climb various mountains in the Tour de France, for example, are available on the internet, a VAM figure gives pro riders a comparison with top riders like Alberto Contador. Try it, but don't get too disheartened by the result!

Ramp test

You'll need a heart rate monitor and a turbo trainer with a speedometer or a power meter fitted to either the turbo or the bike (with the speedo sensor on the back wheel). Try to ensure that conditions for the test are always consistent, using the same bike, gearing and pressure on the rear tyre. A regular ramp test, noted in your training diary, will become an invaluable guide to how your training is progressing.

- Five minutes: Warm up in an easy gear.
- Nine to fifteen minutes: Ride for three minutes, three to five times depending on fitness, while ramping up the speed or power in increments of 2mph or 50 watts.
- Over the last 30 seconds of each three minute ramp: Record average heart rate. You want to get a heart rate that represents your effort at that speed or power output, not a spike or dip i.e. the load is ramped to such a level that only 3 min of effort and no more can be sustained.
- Five minutes: Warm down.

Constant heart rate test

Coming at it from a different angle is a test that does not require maximum effort but records the figures after a set period of time at a steady pace. The idea is to ride at a heart rate that is on the comfortable side of hard, say about 75 per cent of your maximum heart rate (see Maximum heart rate below) for 30 minutes on a turbo trainer.

At the end of the test period, take down the distance covered. Always use the same heart rate, so the further you ride for this same effort indicates an improvement in your fitness. Make sure you add 15 minutes at the beginning and end of the test for a warm-up and warm-down.

TESTS TO ESTABLISH TRAINING ZONES

Fitness tests monitor progress and should give you the confidence that everything is going in the right direction. You only need to pick and repeat one of the tests we've given you to do this.

You must train very specifically to improve your fitness and that means making efforts that are enough to stimulate the various physiological and muscular processes that make you fitter. To do this you need to establish zones of training effort, defined by either heart rate or power, or even by feel, although feel isn't as accurate as the other two, and accuracy is quite important. The two figures you can use are:

- Maximum heart rate or,
- Functional threshold

Maximum heart rate

If you regularly use a heart rate monitor for training and racing, there is every chance that you already know your maximum heart rate, most likely recorded when you have ridden flat out up a hill when warmed up but still feeling fresh. If you have ridden a one-hour circuit or off-road event, you will also have seen big numbers on your heart rate monitor that will be within a beat or two of your max. If not, although it's easier to record your max during a short race, a short session on the turbo trainer, with a heart rate monitor and a speedo, is all you need. But be warned, it's going to hurt.

- After a 10-minute warm-up on low gears, make sure you are feeling comfortable (a cooling fan really helps), fresh and strong.
- Pedalling between 90 and 100rpm, start off at 15mph, then increase the speed by 0.5mph every 30 seconds, maintaining the cadence by shifting up through the gears.

- Keep accelerating every 30 seconds until you can go no faster and are basically riding as hard as you can.
- Your heart rate should be at its maximum at this point. Remember this figure and stop, then warm down for 10 minutes. If you have also noted your maximum speed, you have another benchmark against which you can test yourself at maximum heart rate in future.

Note: Heart rate can be affected by temperature, illness, overtraining and nerves. If your pulse appears higher than normal, that can indicate overtraining or the onset of illness; in those conditions you should postpone the test until you are rested and healthy.

Knowing your maximum heart rate, you can establish some training zones, whether in terms of heart rate or power output, that will help you to develop more specific training schedules. Take your maximum heart rate and calculate training zones as a percentage of that figure, e.g. VO_2 max is 85-90% of MHR, threshold training is at 80-85%, hard endurance training at 75-80%, train for stamina at 70-75% MHR, and recovery should be at 60-70%. The only other figure you need is your functional threshold.

Functional threshold (FT)

Functional threshold is just one click below the level you need to ride at during your fitness tests: it is the hardest you can ride for up to one hour and can be measured in terms of average heart rate, power, speed or feel. Functional threshold as a measurement is one of the most reliable indicators of your aerobic fitness and a great reference point for further improvements.

BIG EFFORT

You need to do the maximum heart rate and functional threshold tests scrupulously and wholeheartedly; you must be well rested and very motivated to do them well. The resulting figures are the foundation stones of your fitness, but, of the two, functional threshold is the most important and the one you should repeat most often. The time to repeat this test is when you feel on top of your training, or that you are not improving any more.

To find your functional threshold you need to follow a similar warm-up procedure as in the tests above and preferably have a safe flat or rolling, but not hilly, course that takes between 20 and 30 minutes. The reason for doing the test over less than one hour is because riding at this pace for one hour is a real race effort and requires the simulation of a race situation. An alternative to a functional threshold test is to take your average power or heart rate from a one-hour time trial or mass start race.

Start your heart rate monitor or power meter recording at the beginning of the main effort, make your effort as hard as you can for the full distance, and stop recording after the 20 to 30 minutes is up. Around 95 per cent of your average heart rate, power or speed for the test will give you a figure close to your functional threshold. From your functional threshold figure, you can calculate the five levels of training effort listed below. We've also included a 'feels like' column so, if you don't have any other monitoring system, you can train on the basis of what a particular effort feels like. Chat level is another good way to judge effort: as you work harder and get more out of breath, your ability to talk is reduced.

Having now established your functional heart rate or power, you can use it to draw up training zones by taking the percentages of the figure and entering them into table 1.2.

TABLE 1.2: TRAINING ZONES

Level	Chat level	Feels like	%FT heart rate	%FT power
1. Easy	Talk freely	Rolling along	69–83%	56–75%
2. Steady	Sentence at a time	Cruising on the flat	84–94%	76–90%
3. Brisk	A few words	Deep breathing going hard	95–105%	91–105%
4. Hard	Occasional word	Attacking flat out	106+%	106-120%
5. Very hard	'Argh!'	Sprinting	Max HR	121%+

RIDER STORY

Wendy Houvenaghel, world track champion in 2008/9 (team pursuit) and Olympic silver medallist in 2008 (individual pursuit), talks about how she started out.

'I took up cycling later than most of the internationals I race against now. Before I cycled I used to run a lot in cross-country and I did the London Marathon too.

'After the marathon I used a bike to help my legs recover. Also, because my husband was a cyclist I had already been to some of his races, so I thought I'd have a go at that.

'But right from when I first started riding I planned my training. I got a coach and followed what he said, did tests and established my training zones and worked at them.

'That approach continued when I became part of the Great Britain team. We do tests and constantly revise our training levels, then train as strictly as possible in accordance with the new information.

'With my coach I plan and set targets, not just in terms of weeks but for each ride I do. I don't think I ever go on a ride without it having an objective, even if it is only to help my recovery from a harder effort.'

The language of fitness

Before embarking on a training programme (*see* chapter 5) it helps to understand the physical processes at work. Knowing which systems are benefiting from the loads you place upon them will help you to gauge how well your programme is working. The body responds to training through changes to the muscles, blood vessels, heart and lungs. How, you might well ask, can a biology lesson help me to become a better cyclist? First, do not be too daunted by the science as it is relatively easy to understand at the level we will be looking at. And second, once you have a grasp of how your body is working, it will enable you to put together a training programme ideally suited to your target events, strengths and weaknesses.

In this chapter we will explain how fast- and slow-twitch muscles work, where they get fuel and energy from, and the best ways to make them stronger and more efficient. How the muscles operate at aerobic (with oxygen) and anaerobic (without oxygen) levels is also integral to the whole process of riding a bike. Just riding around, following the vague notion that you have to 'get the miles in', does not necessarily result in a positive effect on your muscles. That is why it is crucial to appreciate which types of muscle need to be concentrated on if you are to see steady improvements in your power, endurance and speed.

Your heart, lungs and blood vessels are less discriminating than the muscles: physical activity is beneficial to them and they should grow stronger and increase in efficiency with regular training. Once again, however, stress them too gently on long slow bike rides and they will not develop into the strong motor, airbox and delivery system that you'll need for the much higher demands of competition or challenge rides. Ageing can lead to reduced performance in the heart and lungs as well as a loss of certain muscle types. But there are ways to slow the decline and make the most of areas which can remain highly functional well past middle age. Weight training and targeted training sessions can reap remarkable rewards for riders aged 40 and over.

Types of muscle

There are three types of muscle fibre: Type 1, Type 2a and Type2b.

Type 1

Type 1 fibres may not have the glamorous reputation of their more powerful partners, but they are the worker ants in the factory and as such do an invaluable job. Type 1 muscle fibres are thin, their contractions quite weak, although training strengthens them, and they are the first muscle fibres to be recruited at the gentlest levels of cycling. Also known as 'slow-twitch' or 'red' fibres, Type 1s have a smoother, slower contraction rate than Type 2s. That's fine because one of their jobs is to contract many times without fatiguing, enabling you to ride for many hours at a conversational rate. They have a support role to play in harder efforts too.

Type 1 fibres use fats and some carbohydrates as fuels when you ride slowly, at below 60 per cent of maximum effort, but the carbohydrate proportion of that fuel mix increases with effort. Both fuel sources require oxygen, but carbohydrates require more. Easy breathing and conversation means that fat is your main fuel source feeding Type 1 fibres. As soon as you start to breathe harder – to be noticeably aware of your breathing with gaps in the conversation – is when Type 1 fibres switch to using carbohydrates as fuel while calling up assistance from other types of muscle fibre.

Slow-twitch can be a misleading term for Type 1 as the electrical impulse from the brain which jump starts each contraction is, in fact, incredibly fast. It's only relative to Type 2 fibres that Type 1s are 'slow'. Indeed, on a long slow ride the best way to ensure you are using Type 1 muscle is to keep the gears as low as possible and pedal at high revs of around 90rpm.

Type 2a

As you start to ride harder, your breathing gets heavier, the chat stops and the muscles go into a transition phase. Type 1 fibres continue to contract but at the same time other fibres are called up to help out and make a bigger contribution. This is where Type 2a muscle fibres come in. Also known as 'intermediate' fibres, Type 2a contract faster than Type 1 and are five times stronger. However, they also have some of the characteristics of Type 1 fibres in that they can keep contracting for quite a long time and use oxygen and carbohydrates for fuel when working at full force.

Type 2a fibres power short-term harder work. You'll be using Type 2a when you launch an attack in the final miles of a race, go flat out up a hill in a sportive, push yourself to the limit on the last lap of an off-road event, or participate in a short-distance time trial. Carbohydrate is their main fuel source and they rely on aerobic or anaerobic metabolism to process their fuel, depending on how hard you are riding. The switch to anaerobic occurs when your breathing cannot supply sufficient amounts of oxygen, and another process, which doesn't require oxygen to produce energy, contributes to powering your muscles.

It's important to remember that Type 2a muscles begin to operate at efforts up to 80 per cent of maximum aerobic capacity (*see* page 000) and the force with which they contract can be increased by correct training. Type 2a can also make an important contribution to long endurance rides when Type 1 fibres run low on energy.

Type 2b

The prima donna of muscle fibres, Type 2b only come out to play when you need to summon every atom of power from your body in a sprint, metres from the line, the summit or the green light. You will be digging into the final 20 per cent of your maximum when Type 2b fibres are recruited and, at the very top end, there are only a few seconds to make full use of these fast-twitch muscles.

Type 2b are sometimes called 'white' fibres or 'fast-twitch' muscle and, unlike Types 1 and 2a, they are primarily powered by a chemical reaction that occurs within them called the 'phosphate system'. Type 2b are twice as powerful as Type 2a and ten times as powerful as Type 1. You will only get about 10 seconds on full power before Type 2b fibres need a complete rest. In the few seconds that you make an attack, dig hard at the bottom of a hill or sprint at the end of a race, you will be calling upon Type 2b muscle fibres.

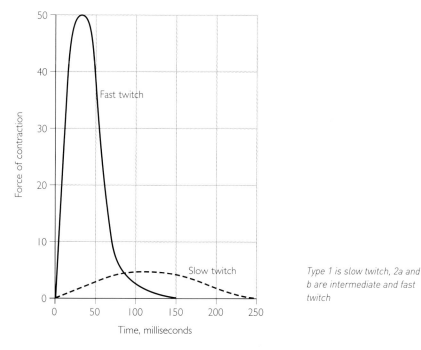

Type 1 is slow twitch, 2a and b are intermediate and fast twitch

Genetics and training

At extreme ends of the cycling scale, with track sprinting at one end and long-distance road riding at the other, the most talented performers will have a genetic advantage over the competition. A leading track sprinter, for instance, might have 75 per cent fast-twitch fibres, compared to a long-distance expert with 40 per cent or even less. It's the luck of the genetics lottery that you might be born with an imbalance in fast- and slow-twitch fibres. Sounds unfair and, yes, it is. The first step in becoming a champion cyclist in any discipline is to choose your parents.

But there's a lot more to it than that. Possessing more fast-twitch fibres than slow ones does not automatically make you a great sprinter. First, you have to choose sprinting as your favoured discipline and love doing it, and you need to be dedicated enough to then train your Type 2 muscles to make the most of their short-term power. To reach a high level with your natural ability will not come easily and your genetics will be worthless if you are not a dedicated athlete. A less genetically enabled rider who trains harder and races with more passion will still beat you, so don't be disheartened if your chosen discipline does not come naturally to you. So much of cycling is about overcoming setbacks and often the rider who faces down each challenge, who battles against shortcomings, is the one who crosses the line first.

Chances are, however, that like most people you will have a roughly equal share of fast- and slow-twitch muscles, both types waiting for you to train them to a high level of efficiency. There will be other riders out there more genetically suited to your favoured discipline, be it sprinting, climbing or long-distance riding, but are they training as hard as you and do they want it as badly as you? That is where the race is won and lost, not on your parents' wedding night.

And there is a free gift from mother nature that will help you in your chosen field of cycling. Type 2a muscles can be trained so that they act more like Type 2b if you do sprint training, and like souped-up Type 1 fibres if your training has an endurance slant. Weight training will increase the size and strength of muscle fibres of all types, as well as making them more efficient: mixing weights with interval training in your programme will strengthen your Type 1 fibres and increase the endurance capacity of Type 2a. Long slow endurance rides will train your Type 1 fibres to work more frugally and encourage Type 2a to take on Type 1 characteristics. However, if you do too much steady riding you will slowly lose the ability to ride really hard, to attack and to sprint.

How the muscles work

The mini-furnaces that power your muscles are the mitochondria. You have trillions of mitochondria inside your muscle fibres, and they are where the numerous chemical reactions take place to produce energy. These are quite complicated, but basically enzymes in the mitochondria act as catalysts sparking off the various chemical reactions that power the muscles.

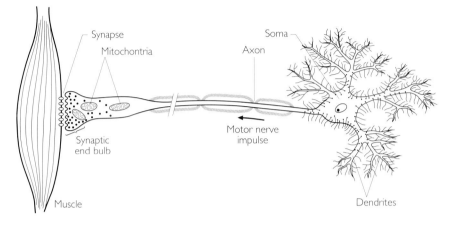

Synapse

Mitochontria

Soma

Axon

Synaptic
end bulb

Motor nerve
impulse

Muscle

Dendrites

Mitochondria power the muscles.

Training or repeated muscular contractions lead to an increase in the number of mitochondria, which in turn increases the muscle's ability to provide energy for itself, and so raises your capacity for work. One way to increase the number of mitochondria is to do long steady endurance rides, but as their production takes place in the 24 hours after exercise it is important to take complete rest days after long rides.

More intense cycling also increases the number of mitochondria, and very recent research has shown that training when glycogen stores and oxygen levels are low is a very effective method of doing this. Try riding for one hour at about 90 per cent of your functional threshold first thing in the morning; or doing a series of longish, six-minute say, intervals after an hour and a half of steady riding, when glycogen stores start to run low. Please note, though, that this latter form of training is cutting-edge stuff and should be used very sparingly and only after you have built up your fitness along the lines specified in this book.

At the end of either session the rider should refuel as soon as possible with carbohydrate and protein – three parts carbohydrate to one part protein, e.g. egg on wholemeal toast, bagel with peanut butter, wholemeal sandwich with lean ham, or a protein energy/recovery bar or shake (*see* chapter 7).

Heart rate

Exercise elevates heart rate (measured in beats per minute) and the heart grows bigger and stronger when stressed regularly in this way. The heart is a pump which, with regular exercise, automatically uprates itself as its chambers grow and walls strengthen. The net result of this is an increase in stroke volume: in other words more blood is pumped to your muscles and organs for each heart beat. One way you can tell if this is happening to you is when your resting pulse decreases. Your maximum heart rate is unaffected by training but a fitter, stronger heart will pump more blood every time it beats – it beats more slowly to supply the same amount of blood at rest.

Maximum heart rate, and percentages thereof, are a useful indicator of training effort, and a heart rate monitor remains one of the most popular ways to gauge the level of effort you are reaching. Maximum heart rate is a personal figure and a higher than average number is not necessarily an indication of ability, increased training or genetic advantage. Maximum heart rate will, however, fall by around ten beats per

TIP

The best time to take your resting heart rate is while lying down soon after waking: a reading from your heart rate monitor, or manually from your pulse, will give you your beats per minute at rest.

decade after the age of 35. There is nothing you can do about that, but maintaining a healthy and fit heart should enable you to perform at your maximum well beyond middle age.

At the other end of the scale, resting heart rate, as well as indicating a steady improvement in the efficiency of your heart, can also be an early warning of illness or overtraining. Resting heart rate should go down the fitter you get and making a regular note of your beats per minute can confirm that you are training right. After recording your resting heart rate first thing in the morning for a few weeks you should get a picture of what your average resting heart rate is. If the measurement shows a 10 per cent increase on a particular morning, it can be a sign that you haven't recovered from the previous day's training, or that you might be going down with an illness. This is a signal that you should either not train that day or do a much reduced session and continue doing that until your heart rate starts to return to its normal level.

Again, resting heart rate is not an indication of how good you are as an athlete, it's a figure that is personal to you and should only be used to assess your physical condition and determine your training zones. And while we're talking about heart rates being personal, never train in someone else's heart rate zones, because the session could work quite differently for you from how it works for them.

Aerobic capacity (VO$_2$max)

Monitoring your heart rate is relatively easy and can be done daily: it is an indirect way to ascertain the capacity of your heart to pump blood around the body. Aerobic capacity, or VO$_2$max, on the other hand, is a measure of how much oxygen your lungs can process when you are working at the top of your aerobic ability. Measuring VO$_2$max, however, is not something you can do at home. It can only be done with sophisticated equipment hooked up to you via a mask while you do a power test on a stationary bike in a sports laboratory.

Knowing your VO$_2$max can give you an idea of your genetic make-up: effective training can show an increase in VO$_2$max but only within the limits that are set down in your DNA. VO$_2$max also drops off with age – about 1 per cent per year after the age of 25. Stay fit, especially if you include proportionately more speed than distance work in your training, and you can hang on to your VO$_2$max figures for much longer.

More importantly, a lab-based VO$_2$max test can yield the power figures and measure lactate levels at which you are working at maximum aerobic capacity. Those figures can then be used to set training zones. Training at your VO$_2$max is the most effective way to build strength and endurance together. At this level both Type 1 and 2a, and to a certain extent 2b, muscle fibres are recruited and, since you are at or very close to your anaerobic threshold (*see* Lactate below), that is increased too.

Luckily, although riding at VO$_2$max is a complicated process within your body (it is as hard as you can go using oxygen as the catalyst for burning glucose as fuel), training at it is quite straightforward and can be done whether you've had a test to ascertain your VO$_2$max or not. You work at your VO$_2$max when you are going as hard as you can

FACT

VO$_2$max is a measure of oxygen utilisation during near-maximal exercise in millilitres per minute per kilogram of body weight (ml/min/kg). Some typical values are:

· Good VO$_2$max: 50 or above
· Olympic rider: 70
· Lance Armstrong: 85
· Miguel Indurain: 88

for three minutes: a very effective session that will help you to achieve your genetic VO$_2$max potential, and hold on to it as you age, would be to do a thorough warm-up followed by three minutes going so hard that you can just hold on for the full 180 seconds and not a second longer.

Start with two or three intervals of three minutes, with five minutes of easy riding between intervals, and then ride easy to cool down. When you can cope with this work, increase to four intervals, and then to five, but don't do more than five. Intensity is everything with this session. Once a week is enough and don't do this type of training throughout the year, just in your build-up to a big race and to maintain peak form.

Efficiency

Now, before you say that Miguel Indurain must be a better cyclist than Lance Armstrong because his VO$_2$max is greater, it isn't quite as simple as that. Although VO$_2$max is a good predictor of performance in endurance sports like cycling, it isn't the only one. VO$_2$max measures the amount of oxygen that a person can use; it doesn't measure how efficiently that oxygen is converted into power at the pedals.

Efficiency is part genetic, part training and part practice. Some people work like lean-burn engines and convert a greater proportion of their oxygen into energy. Some pedal smoothly without any wasteful movements, which also increases efficiency. So does training and, good news for older cyclists, so does the number of years you have been riding. By all accounts Lance Armstrong is a very efficient racer.

Lactate

Taking a measurement of the build-up of lactate in your blood is another test which requires high-tech equipment, an assistant and a sports lab, or at least a portable kit with which you have to use a lancet to prick your own finger to take several samples.

Lactate is a metabolic by-product of exercise. Up to a certain intensity of exercise your body recycles lactate and uses it to create energy. However, above that intensity the recycling mechanisms cannot keep up with lactate production, so it builds up in your muscles. Broadly speaking, when that build-up occurs you cannot increase your exercise intensity, and the build-up can cause you to slow down. When that happens your body then begins to slowly mop up the excess lactate, which it does by using it to provide energy. The intensity at which lactate production exceeds its removal is sometimes called the 'lactate threshold' and sometimes the 'anaerobic threshold'. They are not equivalent, but it is generally accepted that 'lactate threshold' is a good estimate of the 'anaerobic threshold' under most circumstances.

Anaerobic means without oxygen, and it is possible for the body to exercise at an intensity beyond this threshold, but not for long.

Unlike your VO$_2$max, which is a figure fixed by genetics and is only unlocked by training, lactate build-up and the lactate threshold can be raised through training so that you can exercise at harder intensities without crossing the threshold. Also, to a certain extent, you can train your body to cope with exercise intensities beyond the threshold. There are genetic elements to these two facets of fitness, but in both cases correct training is far more important than genetics. How high your threshold is and your ability to cope with excess lactate are very accurate indications of your fitness level.

Lactate and riding effort

Lactate threshold is important in drawing up training zones. If you base these on a lactate test, the accuracy of the zones increases and that can lead to marked improvements in your ability to process lactate at ever greater levels of effort. Your lactate threshold, when levels of lactate in the blood cannot be processed fast enough and accumulate to the point where you need to reduce your effort, is one of the most important areas of training to address and an effective programme can raise it dramatically (*see* chapter 5).

For a non-athlete, the lactate threshold is roughly 50 per cent of their maximum aerobic capacity, while a well-trained cyclist can go to 90 per cent of their maximum before the burning sensation of too much lactate kicks in. There are even one or two gifted pro road racers who can operate at 95 per cent of their maximum heart rate and still process lactate, and some who are able to cope with high levels of lactate that would force anyone else to slow down.

In the lab a lactate test is done by taking a tiny amount of blood from a finger or ear lobe while the subject pedals at ever greater increments of power, for example 25-watt ramp-ups. For an average rider the lactate threshold figure could be around three watts per kilogram (based on the rider's weight). That can then be compared to elite racers at around five watts per kilogram, and anything above six watts per kilogram for professional riders. Lactate threshold can be expressed as both a percentage of VO_2 or a watts per kilo figure.

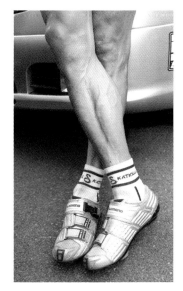

LACTATE MYTHS

· Sore legs at the end of a hard session cannot be blamed on a build-up of lactate. Most of the pain in your legs after training is due to damaged muscle fibres that will heal and become stronger, which is one of the ways you get better at cycling.

· Lactate cannot be responsible for the burning sensation you get in the muscles during a hard effort because it is non-acidic. Tests have shown that lactate operates as a fuel, turning into glucose in the presence of oxygen. It was always assumed to be a waste product because tests showed an excess of lactate when oxygen became scarce.

· Lactate is not harmful – it helps to fuel the muscles and training at high levels of effort should not be avoided due to lactate build-up. Increasing the number of mitochondria in the muscles through endurance training is the best way to raise your lactate threshold.

So why do legs burn during a really hard effort? Simply because they are crying out for oxygen and the pain sends a signal to your nervous system that your legs need as much blood pumping to them as possible.

Power

Of all the ways to measure the effort of a cyclist, power is the most accurate and informative. Since the mid 1990s, when the German SRM power meter was introduced, cyclists have been able to see power outputs while they are riding along, and download them later for further examination. Power meters are expensive but they are more widely available than before and come in various guises, from the SRM system fitted to the chainset, to PowerTap's rear hub with integral power meter.

A cyclist's power, literally the rate of doing work, is most commonly expressed in watts on the readout from a computer linked to strain gauges in the drivetrain depending on which system being used. The SRM system also collects data on cadence, speed and heart rate, all of which can be seen on a handlebar-mounted computer. Information downloaded after the ride shows the whole route expressed as a continual line of watts, along with maximum and average power.

The reason why power has become the benchmark for monitoring an effort is that it concentrates exclusively on how hard you are pushing on the pedals and nothing else. Using speed or time as a gauge is far less accurate, as factors like weather conditions, machine choice and the terrain make an objective assessment imprecise at best. Heart rate can indicate the intensity of an effort but that too can be affected by external factors like temperature, stress and cumulative fatigue. A doubling of your effort will not necessarily result in a corresponding jump in your heart rate. With a power meter you will know, to the nearest watt, whether or not you are working twice as hard as before.

Monitoring power has clear advantages for training, once zones have been set that are relevant to your threshold and maximum power outputs. In a competitive or challenge scenario a power meter is a great way to know how hard you are working and what you have in reserve, if anything! It's also a useful tool if you want to test aerodynamic equipment, cadence and power, and also refine ways to save power in a paceline or bunch situation (see page 000).

Power to weight

The power to weight ratio is a crucial, if not the crucial, figure in cycling. It's simply the power a rider can produce divided by their weight, and is expressed in watts per kilogram. Power to weight is cycling stripped to its basics. Human power is the motive force in cycling, and weight is one of the factors that limits the speed a cyclist can ride at, especially uphill. Think of the power from your body lifting you up: if you are lighter you are easier to lift, therefore you go faster. Wind resistance also holds you back on the flat, but weight is still important, especially when accelerating, because it is easier to accelerate a lighter weight.

The most common power to weight ratio you will see given is the power at functional threshold divided by weight. Of all the things you can measure in cycling, and there are a lot, this is the most important and the ultimate definition of ability in endurance cycling. For men, a beginner who has done some training would expect to put out 2.5 to 2.75 watts per kilogram; for women it ranges from 2.0 to 2.4 watts per kilogram. A top international female racer would put out 5 watts per kilogram, and the Holy Grail of cycling, which can indicate that a male rider will be competitive in the Tour de France, is 6 watts per kilogram at functional threshold.

FACT

You are only as strong as your core.

FOCUS ON

Core Training

Most training for cycling should be done by riding the bike. But there are other activities which help and support cycling, or that can replace it if the weather is bad or you are unable to ride for any reason. One crucial off-the-bike activity that every cyclist must do is core training. Your core is the centre of your body, from your hip muscles, through the glutes and to the abdominal and lower back muscles.

In cycling your core provides the platform against which your legs push. It also links the action of your arms and shoulders to that of your legs. If your core is weak your legs waste energy lifting up your body on each pedal revolution, and much of the input from your arms and shoulders is lost. To picture the effect of a weak core, think about leaning on a backrest and pushing a weight away from you with your legs. If the backrest is rock solid, all your ener gy goes into pushing the weight, but if the back-rest moves, some of the energy in your legs goes into pushing it backwards.

On a bike you are your own backrest, or at least your core muscles are. They need to hold you down into the saddle to form a solid platform to push against. And when you are out of the saddle they must do the same job and resist the force of your legs that tends to lift your body up. This is more difficult and requires a lot of hard work, but next time you see a top pro racer riding out of the saddle, look at the vertical plane of their hips. It won't be moving at all, which means all their leg strength is going into the pedals.

Core strength training can be done without any special equipment other than a carpeted floor. An exercise or Swiss ball greatly increases the range of core exercises that you can perform and a gym will have various pieces of equipment aimed at core training (*see* Chapter 6).

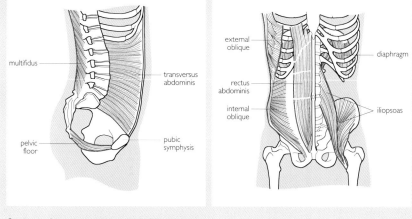

Core muscles – a strong core is vital for cycling.

RIDER STORY

Allan Peiper was a Tour de France rider, the winner of a team time trial stage in that race, and winner of a stage in the Giro d'Italia in 1990. He is a directeur sportif at the HTC-Columbia team of Mark Cavendish, a relatively new team with an incredible attention to the details of rider training. They were one of the first pro teams to employ a strength and conditioning coach, as well as a trainer to oversee their on-the-bike preparation.

Peiper's core training sessions were a revolution in cycling and were cited as one of the reasons for the team's success. Other teams were certainly convinced because they have copied Columbia. Along with the demands of his job, Peiper also keeps himself impressively fit.

'I'm so convinced by the benefits of core training that I cut every training session I do on my bike, or when I can't ride or run, down by 10 to 15 minutes to do some core work at the end of it.

'And since I've been doing it I have definitely felt stronger, and gone faster, on my bike. I feel more solid when I ride, and the stretching and strengthening involved in core work means I don't get out of the team car like a hunchback at the end of a long day driving behind the peloton. Core training isn't just good for your bike riding, it's good for your life too.'

Bike fitting

Establishing the correct riding position, often across numerous machines, is one of those tasks that some cyclists take more seriously than others. It can be a fascinating and ever-evolving diversion for a rider interested in bikes, but for the non-mechanically minded, adjusting and replacing parts is nothing but an irksome chore. What both types overlook is that riding position is not about the bike, nor is it a matter to be guestimated and forgotten. Bike positioning is all about you, your riding comfort and maximising your efficiency. The bike is a tool which needs to be set up and adjusted to suit you. Ignore that and you will almost certainly waste valuable energy and suffer unnecessary discomfort or possibly injury.

A properly set up bike will feel just right every time you sit on it. More than that, it should make you feel poised, coiled even, and ready for action. Whatever the machine, light or lardy, on- or off-road, the setup should not make you feel compromised or unconfident. From a mechanical standpoint, the correct setup will ensure that, from your upper body and arms down through your legs, you can transmit as much power as possible into the pedals.

Even a short bike ride can be uncomfortable on an incorrectly sized bike. Comfort is a setup issue as well as a component one, but whatever your preferences it's also important to ensure that you can avoid unnecessary aches and pains while riding. Get it wrong and you could trigger an injury or aggravate an existing niggle.

As speeds go up, the ability to adopt a position which reduces wind resistance can result in precious seconds gained or energy saved. On a time trial bike the challenge is to find a wind-cheating position without compromising power output. But it's also an important consideration for the road rider, who could be wasting precious watts with an upright riding position.

Finally, fitting the bike to you and setting it up properly should ensure that the machine handles optimally, making it fun to ride and safer too. A balanced riding position, with handlebars and brakes within easy reach, will allow you to descend, corner and brake with confidence.

Saddle height

Science or subjective? There are two schools of thought regarding this hotly debated subject, one side favouring mathematical formulae and angle-measuring, while the other favours a rough and ready method of look and feel. Whichever camp you fall into, you will need at the very least to arm yourself with a tape measure and a plumb line (*see* page 000) to track your saddle-height adjustments while making notes from one bike to another.

Whichever method you use, it is worth approaching the subject of saddle height with common sense and an open mind. Using a formula to compute a precise figure might sound final but it should only be taken as a base setting. From there you can make minor adjustments according to feel and changes related to kit like the cranks, pedals and shoes. Indeed, there are times when micro-adjustments are beneficial to power transfer, handling and recovery from injury.

To determine saddle height mathematically here is one method worth trying (from Ed Burke's *High-Tech Cycling: The Science of Riding Faster*):

- Stand in your cycling shoes and cycling shorts, with feet about 5cm apart, on a flat surface.
- Slide a book tight up against your saddle area, keeping your heels on the floor.
- Measure the distance from the floor to the top edge of the book.
- Take this figure and multiply it by 1.09.
- With the crank arm in direct alignment with the seat tube, the seat height can be set by measuring from the pedal axle to the top of the centre of the saddle.
- This is the highest you should raise the saddle for your measured leg length.

MEASURING ANGLES

If you want to take a further measurement, you will need a goniometer which measures the angle of the knee at the bottom of the pedal stroke. With the saddle set at the correct height, knee angle should be from 25 to 35 degrees. This is measured by aligning the straight edges against the femur and tibia, with the hinge of the goniometer placed against the centre of the outside of the knee joint.

Measuring knee angle using a goniometer.

To determine saddle height without a tape measure:

- Place the bike in a turbo trainer ensuring that the bike is level, with a support under the front wheel.
- Ride comfortably in your normal position.
- Unclip from the pedals and, placing the heels on the pedals, slowly pedal backwards.
- The heels should remain in contact with the pedals through the bottom of the pedal stroke without causing the hips to rock.
- This should result in a slightly lower saddle height than the method above.

Riding the turbo trainer is another way to find an efficient and comfortable saddle height.

Both of the above methods ensure that there is a slight bend in the leg when the foot is at the bottom of the pedal stroke. It is quite possible to arrive at a comfortable seat height this way purely by sight and feel.

Reasons to raise or lower saddle height

All results from the different methods of determining saddle height should be treated as base settings. You may find, from feel and by making a visual judgement, that a base setting is spot on first time. But there are many reasons – such as physical, performance and mechanical considerations – for raising or lowering the saddle. Just make sure that any changes you make are in small increments of about 5mm.

Where possible, the aim should be to replicate saddle height across all your machines. But, as you will see below, this is not mandatory, and it is not hazardous to have a variety of seat heights among a stable of machines used for a variety of disciplines.

Use lower saddle than base setting for:

- Higher cadences, spinning over 90rpm. The pedalling circle extends the legs less and conserves energy in the muscles.
- Fixed wheel on the road or endurance track. Easier on the legs when spinning downhill and suits higher cadences of track racing. Also suits use of shorter cranks (165–170mm) as knee angle is less pronounced.
- Fast pedalling and lower centre of gravity in mountain biking and cyclo-cross (*see* Chapter 4). Cornering and balance on unpredictable ground is easier with a lower saddle. The higher bottom bracket height on an off-road bike also makes this adjustment worthwhile.

Adjusting shoe plates should only be done in small increments.

- Tightness in the back and side of the thigh. This can be relieved by lowering the saddle.

Use higher saddle than base setting for:

- Lower cadences on big gears. With the knee at a wider angle it is easier to push a bigger gear and this position can suit time triallists and sprinters on road and track.
- Knee pain caused by riding with too tight an angle (lower seat). Raising the saddle and increasing the angle can reduce pressure on the patellar tendon.
- Longer cranks (175mm or more). A higher seat height will reduce the amount of knee angle on each rotation.

Check your saddle height if you:

- Swap between pedal systems and shoes. There can be quite significant stack heights (the measurement from the sole of the shoe to the pedal spindle) between different shoe plate systems, especially if you ride with a recessed off-road system like Shimano SPD, and a Look-style road shoe plate.
- Wear different shoes with soles of varying thickness. There can be a difference of up to 8mm between a Look and Speedplay system for instance.
- Bike in winter with thermal tights over shorts. The extra thickness can effectively raise saddle height by several millimetres.
- Fit a new saddle. There is a good chance that the centre-top measurement will be altered compared to your old one.

LEG LENGTH

If there is a discrepancy in leg length it may be necessary to pack out one side of the shoe with a plate or shim (a thin strip made from plastic, cut to sit between the show plate and sole of the shoe). Alternatively you could insert washers of equal thickness between the shoe plate and sole of the shoe, held in place by the mounting bolts. Unequal leg lengths can be natural (lengths of femur and tibia) or due to the result of injury or muscular imbalance. It can also be caused by ankle or foot mechanics, which can be addressed by orthotic inserts in the shoes. To determine which type of imbalance you may have, it is necessary to get checked out with either a scanogram (for static length discrepancies) or radiogram (for functional length discrepancies).

Saddle height should be set for the longer leg, with adjustments made to the shorter side. As well as shims and plates, corrections can be made to shoe plate position. Seeking advice and help from a reputable bike fit expert is recommended before making any significant changes in this area.

Plumb line

After finding a base setting for your saddle height, the next job is to check that your knee is directly over the pedal at the point when the knee is at the centre of rotation, around which it is transmitting the most power. The right-hand side pedal at this point is at three o'clock, horizontal to the ground.

Using a plumb line (string or cotton with a weight at one end), sit on the bike with the pedals horizontal to the ground. Place the plumb line against the front of the knee over the pedal in the three o'clock position. The line dangling vertically should pass very near to the axle of the pedal. Adjust the saddle fore and aft to bring the knee as close as possible to this position.

Time trial specialists and triathletes may favour a knee position a few millimetres forward of this base setting and if you want to try this, you'll need to raise the saddle slightly to maintain the same leg angle. This position may not be as comfortable as the base setting, but for short distance timed events it favours a rider pushing a bigger than normal gear at a lower cadence. On the other hand, pushing with the knee slightly behind the axle line shifts bodyweight further over the rear wheel and can aid traction when riding off-road. By sticking to a base setting, however, you can still shift fore and aft in the saddle and there are longer, flatter saddles on the market which will allow for this.

A plumb line weight dangled from in front of the knee shows the correct alignment with the pedal axle.

SADDLE ANGLE

Once again, the base setting is for the saddle to be as flat as possible and you can check this every time with a spirit level placed along the centre line of the saddle. If the saddle is more curved than usual, it can be aligned by eye against a horizontal line behind the bike.

Women and time triallists may prefer a slight downward tilt of the saddle nose. For women it can relieve pressure on the perineal area and for time triallists it can rotate the body forwards slightly, putting more weight into the aero bars. Angling the nose of the saddle up prevents a rider sliding forwards but it can also result in lower back pain.

For riders with a pelvic imbalance, it's better to adjust handlebar position and height than to play around with the tilt of the saddle. Stretching exercises designed with this in mind are also worth considering (*see* page ooo).

Using a spirit level ensures the top of the saddle is flat.

An all-day riding position should combine comfort and balance with a low frontal area.

Upper-body position

Balance, comfort and aerodynamics are the three key areas to address when determining upper-body positioning on the bike. In effect this comes down to the reach to the bars and, like saddle height, there is a base setting to arrive at before working through the options offered by different bars and brake levers.

The base setting for the upper body should the most comfortable position that the rider can hold while riding as low as possible. For most people this will not be on the drops but somewhere between the hoods of the brake levers and the top of the bend. With the plumb line held on the nose, the line should pass through the centre of the stem.

This may not necessarily result in a flat back, as trying to ride in such a low position would be unsustainable over long periods of time. A line through the back and centre of the head should be roughly parallel to the down tube, and the back should be straight or gently bowed, with no awkward looking bends in it. There can be quite marked differences between riders of different arm and back lengths, and to get the right position you might have to change stems, stem spacers, bars or brake lever positions.

In the cockpit

Modern Ahead-style headsets have made vertical adjustment of the stem less easy and you may find that there is only a small range of adjustment with the spacers provided above and below the stem. The minimalist design of Ahead headsets allow the stem and bars to be sited closer to the head tube, thus allowing for a lower riding position at the front of the bike. Professional team bikes often have the stem slammed as far down the steerer tube as possible, resulting in a very low front end. Beware of copying this trend as it can result in a much greater drop from saddle to bar. If there is little or no vertical adjustment available, it can be possible to flip the stem, altering the angle of rise between the mounting point on the steering column and the handlebars, and gaining a centimetre or two on the high-rise angle side of the stem.

Take measurements from the saddle tip to the centre of the handlebars, and to the lever hoods and drops of the bars too.

Apart from measuring from the tip of the saddle to the centre of the bars, It Is also worth taking a measurement from saddle tip to centre of the lever hoods and centre of your hand position on the drops. You might be surprised at the differences between different bar types and brake lever hand positions. To determine the difference in height between the saddle and the bars, measure from the ground up to the top of the saddle and tops of the bars.

Handlebar width should correspond to the width of your shoulders. A wider bar can be favoured for comfort and more handling feel but it is less aerodynamic and can make filtering in bunches trickier. For off-road, a wider bar is preferred as it allows the rider to make tight turns with greater ease and precision. It also helps to have the bars raised a little for off-road riding, reducing load on the arms and freeing them up for more technical head-up manoeuvres. As speeds are slower off-road, aerodynamics are less of a concern and a more upright riding position is favoured.

Holding an aero tuck takes practice and a strong core.

CORE STRENGTH AND FRONTAL AREA

If there is one compelling reason to work on your core strength, it is the opportunity to hold a low aerodynamic position on the bike. Many riders find it uncomfortable riding on the drops in a low position, even with a conventional road setup.

A stronger core relieves stress on the arms and allows the rider to stay low, reducing the frontal area, for longer. Additional strain can be put on the neck in the tuck position and, alongside core strength routines, stretching exercises to improve flexibility in the neck, spine and hamstrings (see page 000) will help maintain a low position comfortably.

Crank length

Leg length is the main determinant of the length of the cranks, based chiefly on the range of movement that the hips and knees go through from the bottom of the stroke to the top. The longer the cranks, the greater the range of flexion and therefore the potential for aches and pains in the knees and hips.

Personal preference also plays a part, however, and some riders can train themselves to comfortably pedal longer cranks with impressive results. A longer crank exerts greater leverage and is traditionally associated with a slower, big-gear pedalling style.

TIP

Use longer cranks for off-road to provide more leverage and make the most of the power phase of each pedal revolution. Short cranks are easier to accelerate with and have to be used in bunch races on tracks of 250m or less.

TABLE 3.1: TYPICAL CRANK LENGTHS FOR RIDERS

Length (mm)	Applicable to riders
160	Under 5ft
165	Under 5ft 5in and track bikes
170	Short road cranks for riders around 5ft 6in
170–172.5	Standard length cranks for riders up to 6ft
172.5	6ft and above
180–185	Extra-long cranks, as found on mountain bikes, or for riders over 6ft who prefer a slower cadence

Shoe plate adjustment

This is a fiddly job and one that can be confusing when trying to align the shoe plate for the yaw angle (heel out or in) on the pedal. Many shoes come with markings on the sole and these are useful for the initial setup, when you are trying to establish a base setting. Depending on the type of pedal you are using, setting the amount of float will also be a factor.

The base setting should place the ball of the foot directly above the pedal axle, with the shoe plate in the centre of its slot, leaving a half to one centimetre gap between the side of the shoe and the crank. To set the yaw angle, point the tip of the shoe plate at the centre of the toe box of the shoe. Set the float in the middle unless you have already decided to go for a fixed position or a fully floating one.

Adjustment of the yaw angle is a personal preference but you should be guided by your natural foot position, standing and walking. A base setting should place the heels slightly inwards, with the ankle almost brushing the crank. It is not unusual to favour a more heel out position, even on one foot, but it is worth riding in the base setting with the pedal on full float to ensure that you are comfortable pedalling this way. Most pedals will allow for a small range of yaw movement right up to the fully locked setting.

There are numerous reasons to move the ball of the foot either side of the pedal axle.

In front of the axle for:

- Less leverage from the foot and reducing stress on the Achilles tendons and calves.
- Greater ease in controlling foot movement if feet are larger than size 10.
- Pushing big gears – can be a preferred foot position.
- Faster pedal location when remounting in cyclo-cross events.
- Easing pressure on the feet for long-distance riders.

Behind the axle for:

- More leverage from the foot, but places extra stress on the Achilles tendon and calves.
- High-cadence track riding with more flowing ankle movements (ankling).

The ball of the foot should ideally be placed above the pedal axle.

Q-FACTOR

The distance between your feet when clipped into the pedals is the 'Q-factor'. Look down from a seated position and you can see that the legs in effect make a triangle, with the base of the triangle aligned between both axles. On bikes with triple chainsets, especially mountain bikes, the Q-factor can be quite pronounced and a potential source of discomfort in the knees.

In general the smaller the Q-factor the better, and if transferring to a machine with a bigger Q-factor, it may be worthwhile increasing the float setting or riding with shoes that place the heels further in towards the cranks. Some riders with excessive pronation, pigeon toes or leg alignment issues should consider Q-factor as a possible aid to their riding style. Spacers on pedal axles, and pedals with a choice of axle lengths, can also be considered.

Time trial position

Riding a time trial on a low-profile TT bike is one of the most specialist racing disciplines in cycling. And since the advent of tri-bars more than 20 years ago, the constant search for riding positions and ever-more slippery kit continues to fascinate and polarise. From the genius of Graeme Obree, who came up with two of the most aerodynamic riding positions ever devised (both of which were subsequently banned by cycling's world governing body, Union Cycliste International (UCI)), to carbon-fibre TT bikes born in the wind tunnel, it's all too easy to lose sight of the simple basics of TT riding.

Low frontal area

Reducing the frontal area of rider and machine is job number one when setting up your low-profile machine or your road bike with tri-bars. Around 70 per cent of the drag acting on a bicyclist is caused by the rider, with 30 per cent (20 per cent for low profile) down to the bike. When cycling at speeds above 20mph, the aerodynamic drag is so great that 80 per cent of your effort is required to overcome it and maintain the pace. So you can see that it definitely pays to put a lot of effort into perfecting your most aerodynamic riding position.

A carbon fibre time trial bike showing the extreme drop from saddle to bars and a low frontal area.

Riding on the drops on a conventional road bike with drop handlebars can be up to 20 per cent more efficient than riding on the tops. Riding in that position alone can save three minutes over 25 miles against a rider on the tops of the bars. On tri-bars the advantages are even greater – it's roughly another two minutes better than a rider on the drops.

Look at photos of riders in each position and you can see that the more upright the riding position, the greater the area of chest exposed to air blowing into the funnel made by the arms, shoulders and head. You need to brick up that tunnel entrance by lowering the head and bringing the arms closer together.

Comfort

How aerodynamic you can get on the front of the machine, how low you can get your head, and how effectively you can orientate your elbows and hands depend on experimentation and lots of practice, which take time. It's not just the front of the bike which requires adaptation either: by rotating the hips forwards it is also possible to flatten the back even further, creating an upper-body riding position almost parallel to the top tube.

Not many cyclists can achieve this riding position without extensive testing and adaptation gained from regular training rides in the aero tuck. If there is continued discomfort or loss of power, the aerodynamic gains are worthless. An acceptable compromise is to maintain power and comfort while concentrating more on the position of the arms and the head than the back. It's better to feel comfortable and get the power down with a slightly rounded back than it is to flatten your back and rotate your hips but lose power through compromising your leg stroke and breathing.

Note the supportive but aerodynamic arm position of this TT rider.

And don't forget, you still need to see clearly ahead and control the bike while riding in the aero tuck. There is no point contorting yourself into the ultimate tuck if you then have to pop up out of it, losing precious seconds gained, when you are not totally comfortable cornering and descending on the tri-bars.

Arm position

Your base setting for an aerodynamic position on tri-bars should be to support yourself just in front of the elbows, with the forearms at right angles to the upper arms. The upper arm should be vertical to the ground. If you practise the plank as a core training exercise (*see* 000), this is the most comfortable position – with the elbows and forearms on the floor supporting your outstretched body similar to a press-up.

Opening up the arms a few degrees and moving the elbows forwards a centimetre or two will lower your back and head, but this should only be done incrementally. Try the same position in the plank and you will quickly feel the additional load put on your core in this more stretched-out position.

Closing the angle between the upper arms and forearms will raise the hands towards the face and this so-called 'praying mantis' riding position, which effectively channels the air around the open funnel towards the stomach, is undoubtedly a very fast riding position. It falls foul of regulations set by the UCI, however, and is not allowed in any of their sanctioned events.

The elbows should be as close together as you can comfortably get them. There is no point pinching them together if they constrict your breathing or cause discomfort in your upper arms. Research has shown that riding in the correct tuck position should have no effect on a rider's oxygen uptake. The current trend is to angle the forearms slightly inwards, with the hands closer together by about half the distance compared to the spread of the elbows.

Ride your TT bike!

Unless you are racing regularly on your TT bike, and even if you are and are serious about improving, it pays to ride it in training. Getting used to the feeling of riding in an aero tuck position can be done on a normal training ride and it is well worth doing as it programmes the body to adapt to the new position. Wear your normal training clothing for this ride and use a pair of standard road wheels and tyres to avoid wear and damage to your aero TT wheels.

TIME TRIAL REGULATIONS

Cycling's world governing body has considerably tightened its rules in recent years, in an attempt to banish extreme riding positions as well as rein in advances in aerodynamic equipment. Here are the key UCI regulations governing riding position and kit for time trialling.

· Forearms must be positioned in a horizontal plane and the extension designed in such a manner that the rider can adopt and maintain a regulatory position for the entire duration of the event.

· The rider's position for the time trial on the road and for the pursuit on the track is defined by two measurements of the bicycle: the position of the tip of the saddle behind the bottom bracket (-5cm minimum) and the advanced position using the extension (+75cm maximum).

· The saddle position is measured from the tip of the saddle to the vertical plane passing through the centre of the bottom bracket axle. The advanced position is measured along the handlebar extension (overall length) from the vertical plane passing through the centre of the bottom bracket axle.

· The profile of the extension must conform to the 1:3 ratio (an aerofoil section, a wing-shaped frame spar or part of an aero handlebar, cannot be three times wider than it is deep).

· The extension shall be fitted with handgrips (point of contact for the hands). These may be located on the handlebar extension horizontally, inclined or vertically.

· Extensions that are raised or arc-shaped are not authorised.

Wheels, skinsuit and helmet

Setting up your TT bike for the ideal aerodynamic riding position will save about two minutes over a rider on the drops on a conventional bike in a 25-mile time trial. That is the result of some serious tinkering with your position and, of course, the effort of riding the distance.

But there are at least another two, yes *two*, minutes up for grabs, with no effort at all, if you and your bike take advantage of aero clothing and equipment. Chester Kyle tested various items and calculated the advantage in seconds to be gained over a conventional bike and rider in a 25-mile time trial at 23mph (37km/h).

TABLE 3.2: TIME ADVANTAGES GAINED USING AERO CLOTHING AND EQUIPMENT

Item	Advantage (sec)
Front disc wheel	66
Aero helmet	47
28 aero-spoked front wheel	44
Rear disc wheel	33
Short-sleeve skinsuit	29
No bottle and cage	26
Aero brakes and levers	18
Aero bottle and cage	15
Shoe covers	13
Aero chainset	5

TIP

A wind tunnel test can pay dividends for keen time triallists, potentially gaining many more seconds than just buying the latest disc wheel.

FOCUS ON

Getting advice

One good thing about the human body is that it is adaptable. However, with cycling that can sometimes be a double-edged sword. The perfect position is always arrived at by adapting your bike to you, but what can happen is that you adapt to the bike.

You can set up your position following good guidelines and never have a problem, simply because your body adapts to the position you have arrived at. But general guidelines, even the ones we give here, don't take account of individual differences. There might be something about you, such as an extra-large femur to tibia ratio, that if catered for in your bike setup could allow you to get more power down to the pedals. This is where professional bike fit systems come in.

You'll see them advertised in the cycling press. You go for a consultation with a qualified person who takes various measurements and will put your bike on a rig, or he will have one from which readings can be taken and then applied to your bike. The net result is a setup that puts you in the optimal position for your body's levers – your legs, arms and upper body – which you are asking to put the maximum power into the pedals. It's a setup that should also take into account any idiosyncracies.

The thing to focus on is that bike position is a big factor in how fast you go, in terms of both maximising your power output and reducing the drag created by your riding through the air. If you get both sides of this equation right you will go faster for no extra effort, and that is worth a lot of training.

RIDER STORY

Chris Boardman, 1992 Olympic champion, three times yellow jersey winner in the Tour de France (1994, 1997, 1998) and the world hour record holder (1993, 1996, 2000).

'During my racing career I travelled a lot and was always getting new bikes. The problem with travel was that my bikes were always being dismantled and put back together again. I marked my handlebar and saddle positions on my bike, but believe it or not there was one time, at the world championships in Norway, when I got on my bike to ride the pursuit semi-finals and as soon as I started I realised my saddle was too high. I'd made a mistake.

'I had marked the seatpost which I had used on another, bigger bike a couple of weeks earlier and looked at the wrong mark when I put mine together. It was then that I decided to take measurements of all the key distances on my bike and record them on drawings, one for track, one for road and one for time trial.

'Nowadays road bike positions are very different to time trial positions, so my other tip is to use this turbo exercise when you swap between the two, or when you make any changes in either position. It will help you get used to the new position quickly.

'Put your bike on a turbo and warm up with brisk pedalling for 15 minutes, pedalling at 90–100rpm. Now, get into the position you race in and choose a big gear and resistance that allows you to pedal at only 50–60rpm.

'Go at your maximum for five to six seconds, but just use your core and legs to power the bike, don't lunge all over the place. Recover for 24 seconds and do five to six seconds at max again. Repeat this 18 more times then ride easy for five to ten minutes. Then repeat another 20 max efforts.

'Do this two or three times per week on top of your training, or as part of it if you are pushed for time, and you will quickly adapt to your new position.'

Riding technique

What makes cycling such an absorbing sport is the way it combines the highest levels of athleticism – right up there with the fittest people in any sport – with the deftness and daring of a motorsport competitor. You can be the fittest person in the world but if you can't go around a corner you'll always be a nervous rider.

Without question the primary reason to take seriously the technique of cycling is that riding a bike is a sport which mostly takes place on open roads where the hazards are known to all. Put simply, mastering the most elementary actions will greatly reduce the likelihood of crashing. If you are not a confident bike handler – and there are some very fit cyclists out there who are less than competent in that department – then you owe it to yourself and your continued good health to upgrade your skills.

Riding safely is not boring. Falling off is boring – spending days, weeks or even months losing fitness while you recover is something that no cyclist ever likes to repeat. We have all been there and most of us were lucky enough to look back on a temporary sabbatical from the bike; but we all know of cyclists who have never returned from injury, and sometimes, tragically, worse things have happened.

You won't win many races or finish many challenge events if you keep throwing yourself over the bars. Master the skills of staying in the saddle and you can move on to honing your handling techniques: these are the kinds of skill that can help you to shave seconds from your times, make passes on rivals, master climbs and descents, and ride in groups and pacelines. With each skill learned you will also need to sharpen your perception of danger and make cool-headed decisions based on the level of risk.

In this chapter we will take a look at the skills and techniques which will help you ride safer and faster. Riding safely and handling your machine with skill and verve are two things which a cyclist can enjoy perfecting throughout their cycling career. Efficient pedalling is another important skill to master and something that you need to attend to at the earliest opportunity – it's the one interface between you and the bike from which the mechanical morphs into the athletic. Understanding the dynamics of the pedal stroke and the significance of cadence is essential if you want to ensure that the power you are producing reaches the back wheel as efficiently as possible.

Safety first

It might sound obvious but whenever you go out riding, safety should rank number one on your list of priorities. The only time that other considerations come close to the top spot is when you are competing in a traffic-free environment, when the consequences of a manoeuvre going wrong might not be as serious as on the open road. Even then you should ask yourself if there is a safer way to take the final corner or make a race-winning attack.

Staying alert by maintaining an awareness of the conditions every minute of your ride will ensure that you are primed and ready to react to the unexpected. Most of your attention will be taken up by the presence of motor vehicles and that means everything from cars, vans, trucks and buses to motorcycles. All behave in different ways. Developing an ear for each type of vehicle – the engine sounds and speed – can greatly help you anticipate how close they might pass when they approach from behind.

As the vulnerable party, your only sane option when mixing with motorised traffic is to ride defensively as much as possible, giving yourself enough room in every scenario to steer or brake yourself out of danger. Do not rely on reactions alone to extricate yourself from a hazardous scenario. You might get away with it a few times, but there is no substitute for anticipating a problem and pre-empting a split-second risky escape trick. Ride defensively but do not apologise for your right to share the road. Be confident and assertive when you need to be, without crossing the line into arrogance or aggression. It's better to take your rightful place in the road, where other vehicles can see you, than to weave in and out of parked cars pretending that you don't exist.

Confidence in your machine is vital. Make sure your brakes are as good as they can be, with smooth-running cables, quality brake blocks and levers adjusted to suit your riding position. Tyres with plenty of life in them, pumped to correct pressures, are also confidence boosters, especially on poor roads. Remember that there is a time and a place for pushing your luck on the bike, and nine times out of ten it's not when you are out training and riding on the open road.

Safety do's

- Ride defensively but confidently and assertively in traffic.
- Think about the type of road you are on and its character.
- Wear colourful or hi-vis tops in low-light conditions.
- Anticipate a risky scenario and avoid or slow down in advance.
- Develop an ear for the speed and type of traffic coming from behind.
- Wear a helmet, especially when riding in heavy traffic or off-road.
- Remember, ultimately there is only one person responsible for your own safety: you!
- Try to make eye contact with other road users – you cannot be certain as to what they will do until you confirm that they have seen you.

Safety don'ts

- · Rely on reactions alone – one day they will let you down.
- · Daydream or fail to concentrate when making a manoeuvre.
- · Neglect to maintain your brakes or tyres.
- · Treat the open road the same as a traffic-free race circuit.
- · Be arrogant or aggressive.
- · Jump lights or ride on pavements.
- · Assume that another road user knows or cares about you or your sport.
- · Check out your reflection in shop windows!

Advanced handling

Cornering

Scything through a corner on a fast descent or while powering along on the flat has got to be one of the greatest joys of bike riding. It's one of those thrills which never fails to put a smile on your face and it's the closest thing you can get to flying while still in contact with the ground.

Cornering at speed is not just fun, it's one of the many little aspects of cycling which, if done well, can maximise your time over a given course. Another way to look at it is that a cyclist who knows how to go around a corner can take a few metres or a fraction of a second out of less competent cyclists on every fast corner. In a time trial the margins could equate to multiple seconds: in other words, the difference between first and second place. In a road race one corner in the final 100m could make the difference between winning and losing.

Cornering, especially getting around downhill bends, is often seen quite simply as a test of bravery. How many times have you heard another rider described as a 'crazy descender' or 'fearless in the bends'? It makes bike handling sound like the preserve of brave warriors or unhinged characters. In fact, the best descenders are often not the ones covered in scars. Crazy bike riders are few and far between: crashing a bike because you are going too fast is not something anyone likes to make a habit of. It usually ends up hurting, a lot.

Good bike handling is not a god-given talent: cool-headed students of the art can reach the highest levels of bike riding technique and they are often the riders who crash the least of all.

Apex of a corner

This is the point at which an imaginary racing line drawn around a bend touches the inside of the corner. The apex represents the point at which the line comes closest to the inside of the bend, between the entrance and exit of a corner, and is the smoothest and therefore fastest line for a cyclist. Unless the corner is a perfect curve, the apex will not be found at the furthermost tip on the inside of the bend. It will be either to one side or the other depending on how 'closed' or 'open' the exit to the corner is.

Do not confuse the racing line with the shortest line. There is no apex around the shortest line, as that is one which just hugs the inside of each corner. So why not tuck into this tightest line? It may be shorter than the racing line but you will find that you have to take it much slower to get around, with more braking and accelerating on the entrance and exit. It's much faster to use as much of the road as possible to open out the corner by using a more flowing, though slightly longer, racing line.

On a closed road, a circuit or off-road bend, the apex can literally be 'clipped' each time, with the rider using as much of the ideal line around the corner as is available. On the open road, safety factors and the direction of traffic will determine whether or not the apex can be clipped, or used merely as a reference.

Vanishing point

Approaching a fast corner for the first time, one way to gauge your entry speed is to look at the point where the road tapers away from sight. Like the tip of a nose, or an up-ended V, if the vanishing point appears not to be moving, or is moving very slowly, the bend is tight on the exit and you need to slow down. If the vanishing point moves progressively away from you, smoothly opening up your sightline as you progress through the corner, then it's a faster bend that requires less braking on the entry to mid-corner.

Bend types
Constant radius

Found on well-engineered roads, a constant radius bend describes a smooth arc with clear sightlines on the entrance and exit, with the apex located in the centre of the inside of the bend. The vanishing point moves progressively all the way into the corner and this type of bend can be taken very fast with little or no braking.

Dual radius

The dual radius is a long double bend with a flatter middle section. The racing line clips two apexes, one on the entrance and one on the exit. It is a tricky corner to get around for the first time as it has two vanishing points and two apexes.

Hairpin

A tight bend, the hairpin demands a wide line on entry, apexing further around the inside than on a constant radius corner. It is often found on well-engineered mountain passes and has a vanishing point that moves very slowly on entry, requiring significant braking. A skilled rider can take a hairpin bend on a descent very fast, braking hard on the entry and leaning the bike right over through a late apex.

Blind

A blind bend is any bend without a sightline through to the exit from the entrance: basically you cannot see what's on the other side and need to scrub the speed. As you speed towards a blind bend, the vanishing point will not start to move away from you until you are deep into your breaking zone in the first third of the bend. It is a risky bend to take fast, especially on the open road where there's a very real chance of running wide on the exit.

If a course has a series of bends I ride them a few times to pick the line where I will have to brake and accelerate the least. Then in the race I make a big effort before and after the bends, but use them to recover because my line means I'm not wasting energy braking and accelerating.

Fabian Cancellara, time trial world and Olympic champion

U-turn

The slowest type of bend, the U-turn is the only one which requires the rider to literally steer the machine around it, having braked to a speed at which the machine is virtually upright through the corner. In a criterium race a U-turn bend is not a hard bike handling manoeuvre but you will be cursing this bend the 30th time you have to sprint out of one!

Chicane

Like a dual radius bend but in micro form, the chicane bend is most often found on motor-racing circuits, where it is designed to slow down racing cars and motorcycles. The narrowness and slower speeds of a bicycle mean that most chicanes can be taken flat out by following the shortest line between the apexes of the obstacles on the entrance and exit. All it may require is a positive shift in body weight from one side to the other, flicking the bike one way then the other without any appreciable cornering input.

Roundabout

A roundabout is a corner with one entry, multiple exits and different apexes, depending on which exit is to be taken. Roundabouts are constant radius corners so once you know which exit to take, you can determine whether to choose a wide (any exit between six and ten o'clock) or straight (between three and twelve o'clock) line. If the road is open to traffic then you must obey the rules of the road and put safety above any notions of cornering. Roundabouts can also be slippery (diesel spills and rubber deposits), uneven (heavy braking by motor vehicles can ripple the Tarmac) and off-camber – all these demand additional vigilance and caution.

Cornering and downhill technique

To cornering technique you could also add descending, because these handling skills on bends only really come into play when the speed goes up and it's on a descent that cyclists hit the highest speeds. It's on downhill corners where you will be drawing upon most, if not all, of your bike handling skills, not to mention your nerve! Anyone can go fast in a straight line – it's in the corners where the keen student of bicycle dynamics gets the chance to dazzle.

Position

If your bike is set up correctly you should be balanced and comfortable in a variety of riding positions. It's essential that you feel relaxed and confident on the bike, with a riding position which allows you to easily reach and operate the brakes without compromising your balance on the machine or the view ahead. Avoid tensing-up your arms and shoulders – remind yourself to keep your arms slightly bent and shoulders loose. You can react quicker this way and will save energy – both physical and nervous.

Get used to your position on the bike when going into corners, either in a tuck or with hands on the brake hoods. It should feel entirely natural to 'pop up' into your braking position as you enter a corner, even if that just means you shift slightly more squarely into the saddle and lift your head to allow you to look as far through the bend as possible.

Think ahead

A good cyclist will always be thinking about the road they are on – how it is likely to unfold or if the surface will change. An appreciation of the terrain and types of road through it can help a rider predict the conditions ahead.

Riding in a country like the UK with an old network of lanes and mostly short climbs, many of them hedge-lined, requires a lot more caution than cycling on more modern European roads with smooth surfaces, engineered corners and long sightlines. Alpine descents, often with multiple hairpins, can also be anticipated and tackled with an almost robotic efficiency, once you have mastered your technique on the first few. Descents with multiple hairpins can be a lot of fun and a great way to hone your technique.

Lean don't steer

You don't steer your bicycle through a corner, you steer it by leaning into the bend and aiming your whole body and the machine towards the apex. The bike turns thanks to a process called counter-steering, which, believe it or not, is a subconscious act by which you actually turn the bars very slightly away from the direction of the corner. This causes the bike to lean, imperceptibly, the opposite way to the bars, tipping the machine into the corner.

Keep your body still and allow your straightened leg on the offside of the bike to take a little of the weight off your behind. It's not obligatory to stick your inside knee out, Moto GP-style, but it can lower your centre of gravity very slightly if you are leant right over.

Cornering in style with head up, left leg straight, arms slightly bent and fingers on the brakes.

Look where you are going

Look at a photo of a professional rider entering a fast bend and chances are you will see that he has his head up and is looking at a slight angle towards the vanishing point of the bend. Looking a few metres in front of the bike may feel like the safest thing to do, as many riders worry about the road surface and the catastrophic dangers of gravel or potholes. If you are travelling at speed, however, you will leave yourself only a fraction of a second to react to a hazard in the road surface.

It's much better to practise lifting your head slightly and forcing yourself to look as far into the bend as possible, searching for the apex and exit and scanning the surface for irregularities. It may feel odd at first but with practice you will find that looking ahead not only makes you faster, but also gives you more time to make a safe change of line to avoid a surface irregularity.

Braking

Hard braking on a bicycle should be done with the bike upright, using two-thirds front brake to one-third back. In the wet the balance should be equal between front and rear. A road bike with modern brakes and good tyres can be braked surprisingly hard in the dry. It's highly unusual to see a rider crash due to a front wheel lock-up.

A mountain bike with disc brakes and suspension fork can be braked even harder, more like a motorcycle, thanks to a bigger contact area provided by the front tyre and the forgiving nature of the fork which takes the initial sting out of the braking force by diving then tracking the ground without 'chattering'.

On the entrance to a corner it's important to scrub off most of the straightline speed before making the turn. It is possible to enter the corner on the brakes but it's best to be progressively letting them off as you do so. All braking should be done smoothly, with at least two fingers on the levers while riding in the drops.

In the wet

Good news – no one expects you to ride like a hero when it's raining. Bicycle riding is not like motorsport in this respect, where every competitor is expected to push almost as hard as in the dry. Cyclists do not pit to change tyres over to full wets, they must make do with what they have got and, as a result, the relative speeds in corners and on descents is considerably lower.

The other good news about wet weather riding is that it requires the same techniques and lines as riding a bicycle in the dry, only with double helpings of smoothness and anticipation. Get it right, stay relaxed and focused and you can ride surprisingly fast and safely in the wet. Remember: ride smooth.

When it goes wrong

In slow, out fast. Keep that in your head and you will negotiate most corners safely and smoothly. If in doubt about the type of bend, it is always best to slow right down before you begin the turn itself. Getting around a corner safely must be your absolute priority when riding on the open road, not only in training but also in competition.

Now and again, however, you might be riding on a closed circuit, on closed roads or off-road with little chance of meeting someone coming the other way. On those occasions you may enter a corner with a little less caution than on an open road, and it's in this situation that you need to have something in your skills locker for when it all goes wrong. You have two options if you find that you have entered a corner too fast.

1. Lean the bike over further

Most riders are worried about leaning the bike over too far when in fact the machine can comfortably hold a line with more lean angle. Have faith in the bike, lean it over a bit more and you stand a good chance of making it through the corner (and leaving the rider behind you several lengths behind). You cannot touch the brakes when at an extreme lean angle as grip is at a premium and there's no margin for an extra loading. If you go down you will slide along on one side into the opposite lane, possibly without hitting anything and suffering more from the abrasion than the impact.

2. Sit it up and brake

The bail-out option requires sitting the bike up in the corner, hitting the brakes as hard as you dare and doing everything you can to avoid an impact. Sometimes you can get lucky here: an open farm gate and grassy field beyond is the Holy Grail. Even trees might be avoided by quick reactions. If it's a rock face on a mountain descent, or even worse, a low guardrail with a drop to the unknown below, lock everything up and hit the deck before you get there. It's going to hurt, but at least the ambulance will find you.

Fast pedalling

After learning to balance a bicycle from an early age, turning the pedals comes a close second on the list of tasks when it comes to riding. Right from the start we learn that it's the forward motion of the machine which enables us to stay upright. Remember the image of a child pedalling furiously away on a tiny bike as he or she wobbles along on their first ride?

The balancing part of cycling really is one of those things that you never forget. Once you have cracked it for the first time that's it – you can ride a bike for ever. But while pushing on the pedals might also sound like simplicity itself, there's an art to transferring your power through the pedals and cranks, and it's a skill that can endlessly delight and fascinate. Apart from the pleasure to be had from the feeling of your feet spinning away beneath you, pedalling correctly is the only way to ensure that you transfer the most power from your legs, enabling you to train and race to the best of your ability.

FACT

One horsepower is the equivalent of 746 watts.

Cadence

More revs equals more power. That is how a petrol engine operates and the same principle applies to a pedalling cyclist. For conclusive proof try to count the revs of a track sprinter – actually don't bother, you won't be able to count 160 revs per minute fast enough! At that rate of pedalling, a track sprinter can produce up to 2,000 watts, which is around the maximum that a cyclist can produce in a single sustained burst.

Fast pedalling is the equivalent of lifting a small weight multiple times, in preference to a big weight a few times. It's a lot easier to lift the small weight quickly and often than it is to put additional stress on your muscles trying to lift the big weight a few times. To get a chunk of work done on the bike it's better to work towards it in small manageable bites than risk overloading yourself with a few mighty lunges. A fast, flowing cadence is not just the best way to maintain high power outputs. In a race situation it is much easier to accelerate by quickly increasing the revs in a given gear than it is to slowly wind up the speed on a bigger gear. You might be able to do it once or twice, but the extra load of the bigger gear will start to tell and before long you will be at the mercy of faster reacting and accelerating rivals on smaller gears.

In training, a faster cadence is the only way you can effectively perform short interval sessions. You can accelerate faster and complete multiple cycles of effort if you get the balance right between leg speed and power. Fast pedalling at low loads is also the best way to train your Type 1 muscles during the endurance phases of your training, when the objective is to improve blood flow to the limbs, oxygen processing and the efficiency of using fuel.

KNOW YOUR CADENCE

Count each time one pedal completes a revolution for thirty seconds. Double the figure to find your cadence in revolutions per minute (rpm).

How many revs?

There is a downside to fast pedalling and it's quite a big one. Oxygen consumption is raised, resulting in increased heart rate. For an advanced or competitive cyclist this may not be devastating news, but it does explain why going faster is not simply a case of pedalling until you black out. There is a band of fast pedalling cadences, from around 70rpm to 110rpm, along which you need to feel comfortable while balancing muscle stress with oxygen intake and heart rate.

It is a given that fast pedalling is the way to go for a competitive rider. That is why it is so important to constantly train your cardiovascular system with fast pedalling training. It may feel strange if you are used to a lower cadence, but in time it will feel completely natural to spin the pedals with practised ease.

Cadence choices

Find the fast cadence that suits you best: for time trialling and climbing it can be at the lower end of the zone, while for off-road and short circuit racing, speeds in three figures can suit. A good way to build a faster cadence is on the turbo trainer or on a fixed wheel bike. However, don't get too fixated on actual numbers.

Cyclists produce more power at faster cadences but there are optimum revs per minute that suit particular body types. For example, Lance Armstrong is always cited as an example of what can be done if you speed up your pedalling, but Armstrong isn't all that tall, not by modern standards, so his legs aren't as long as some.

It's easier to pedal quickly if your legs are shorter. In fact the optimal way to increase power from a short lever is to increase revs per minute. That doesn't work with a long lever, or in a cyclist's case if their legs are long. Long-legged riders should pedal a bit slower, taking advantage of their lever length (in a cyclist's case their thigh), to provide more push in the power phase (*see* below) of each pedal stroke.

Power cycle

When you are wearing cycling shoes that lock onto the pedals it is tempting to try to apply power through the pedals all the way around the revolution. For many years it was assumed that trained riders gained extra power by pulling up on the pedal, from six o'clock through to twelve. Pushing the knee towards the bars at the top of the pedal stroke and 'scraping' the foot at the bottom accounted for the top and bottom of the pedal cycle, while the real power phase came in between from one to five o'clock. In fact, studies revealed that the 'pull' identified in trained riders was merely their ability to unload their 'up' leg so that it caused less resistance to the power provided by their 'down' leg.

Tests have shown, however, that by far the most effective segment of the power stroke is between two and four o'clock, with negligible outputs everywhere else. Three o'clock is where maximum power is applied, when the knee should be positioned directly above the pedal axle. The art of pedalling is to apply the most force at three o'clock as progressively and smoothly as possible. Elite riders tested at 100rpm at close to full power demonstrate this well, with all the power in the two to five o'clock zone.

Max power is applied, as shown here, when the crank is parallel to the ground.

There can even be a slight negative output from seven to ten o'clock as the resting leg pushes down on the pedal while the other leg is going through its power phase. This negative pressure is so small that it is not a significant drain on power. From eleven to one o'clock there is no power output, positive or negative.

Practising skills

Think about every corner you take on every ride. Look at it, assess it and pick the right line through it. Good criterium riders will ride corners, especially the final one, at race speed during their warm-up to get their lines perfectly right. Good time triallists do the same for a time trial course.

Think about your pedalling. One-leg drills on a turbo trainer really help you develop a smooth and economic pedal action. Just unclip a leg, rest it on a chair and pedal with the other leg, using the angle of your foot to push and pull the pedal around. Do one minute then use the other leg and unclip the one you've just used.

One handy tip for improving your bike handling is to ride off-road in the dry on slick road tyres. There are no knobbles to help your tyres grip, so the way you handle your bike must be extra delicate. The lack of grip teaches you how to distribute your weight on the bike through a corner, and it forces you to pedal smoothly, especially out of the saddle, because if you don't you'll suffer from wheelspin.

RIDER STORY

Russell Downing, Team Sky pro, is one of the fastest criterium riders in the pro peloton.

'Cornering is part practice and experience and part instinct. Experience teaches you the right lines, but instinct tells you where the limits of tyre adherence are. Don't panic if your tyres slip a little. Leaning more, and moving your hips and shoulders a little can help bring it back. It's a subtle and unconscious movement, but it's saved me a few times.

'Lean your bike to begin the corner, have your inside leg up and the outside one down, and shift your weight over that outside leg and arm. Keep your head low but upright as that stops you getting disorientated.

'The point of your chin should be at 90 degrees to the floor. Crouch low, and get lower if you feel you are coming off line. Cornering fast is all about getting your centre of gravity as low as possible.

'Press harder on your outside leg too if you are coming off line. Sit in the middle of your bike, not forward or back, because you want your weight even over the front and back wheel.

'As you come out of the corner let the bike come back up, but get back on the power early. Experience is the only thing that can tell you how early though.

'The last thing about bike handling, and this isn't to do with cornering but it's a pet gripe of mine, is when you get out of the saddle take your bike with you. So many people don't. They get out of the saddle for a hill, but when they do they stop pedalling for an instant, then start when they are out of the saddle.

'What happens if you are following behind is that their bike slows, so in effect it comes back at you. It causes crashes because it creates a bigger and bigger reaction down the line.

'Get out of the saddle with one smooth movement but keep pressing down on the pedals as you do.'

Endurance

It's not so long ago that cyclists used to put their bikes away at the end of the season, then wait three months until the new year before digging out a heavy winter hack from the shed for another two months' dismal plodding around the lanes. In those days 'The Winter' was a dank tunnel entered with a heavy heart. Winter represented such a long break from fast training and racing that you never quite knew in what condition you would emerge from the other end. It was pretty much taken for granted that the post-Christmas cyclist would be an overweight, unfit and generally sloth-like individual.

Forward-thinking coaches began to advocate what today is called cross training: non-cycling activities, like running, weight training and skiing, which encouraged the use of non-cycling muscles and honed the senses of balance and co-ordination. From that came the realisation that a short break was all that was required at the end of the summer season, just so long as the training that followed was fun and full of variety. Putting on weight was questioned too – why not use the winter to lose that extra kilogram which slowed you on the climbs the previous summer?

These days it feels as if winter hardly exists at all, and it's not all down to milder weather and global warming. For racing cyclists the off season has been influenced by the globalisation of professional cycling, which means that the pros can finish racing in the Tour of Lombardy in Italy in mid October, then barely three months later reconvene for the first big race of the following season, Australia's Tour Down Under in the third week of January. A four-month off season for non-professional riders is now the norm.

More relevant is current thinking by cycling coaches who advocate training programmes covering 12 months of the year, with similar levels of physical activity through the winter as in the summer months. Riding the bike is not something that you need to take a break from: on the contrary, it's positively encouraged. It's the routine that needs freshening up, as the most important part of the winter tunnel is coming out of the other end fit, healthy, light and full of enthusiasm.

In this chapter we will show you how to create a winter training programme, explaining the five training zones that will help you maintain a good balance of endurance and power right from the off.

Training zones

There are numerous ways to break up your training zones into chunks measured by power, heart rate or perceived level of effort. The idea of training zones comes from the fact that at different levels of effort, different systems in your body are being trained, from fat burning to high-power fast-twitch muscle contractions. For ease of use and lack of confusion we are going to suggest five easily understood zones which cover every level of effort and represent all the zones you will need for a 12-month training programme. Ways of determining the five training zones from power, heart rate and perceived level of effort are covered in Chapter 2.

Level 1: Easy

Easy riding is a very low level intensity effort used for long (two hours or more) solo or group rides at a very steady and sociable pace. It is also the best way to warm up and cool down, using low gears and pedalling at 90rpm plus. Riding easy is the high-volume component of endurance training and is the best way to 'bond' with your bike. Long easy riding also tunes up your engine, growing the heart, blood vessels and mitochondria and creating a leaner burn mix of glycogen and stored fat.

Level 2: Steady

Steady riding comes in at the quality end of endurance riding and this zone, using slow-twitch Type 1 and intermediate Type 2a muscle fibres, is ideal for time-hungry cyclists who can fit in a two-hour endurance ride but struggle to do three- or four-hour sessions. In the steady zone you can still hold a conversation but you'll need to concentrate, and the extra effort required for hills and little accelerations will elicit not much more than a grunt! This could be your sportive pace, or the speed that you would be riding at during a lull in a road race.

Level 3: Brisk

The no-talking zone – the upper part of brisk riding – is your time trialling pace and demands total concentration, deep breathing and top technique. These efforts go right up to and into the functional threshold, where aerobic meets anaerobic power, and can be monitored on the bike using heart rate or power.

The bottom half of the brisk zone is known as a training 'sweet spot', as riding at these intensities requires a physical level of effort that is sustainable for one hour or more and is the best way to grow mitochondria and raise your lactate threshold levels and maximal lactate steady state pace. Make no mistake, brisk riding is high-quality training, almost mimicking a race effort, and it requires planning and space around it for rest and recuperation.

Level 4: Hard

At the hard level of intensity you can only ride for up to 10 minutes and in training this equates to intervals. In a competitive scenario riding hard would equate to the effort you need to make to break away from the pack, bridge across to another group, attack up a climb or make a fast start in an off-road race. This zone is where you can make small increases in your VO_2max, increase your cardiac output and make near-full use of your Type 2a muscle fibres.

Level 5: Very hard

Sprinting, basically, is all you can do at the highest intensity level. You will only be able to sustain a very hard effort for 60 seconds maximum.

Building an endurance base

Endurance is the bedrock of any cycling programme and if you want to maintain your form and handle increasing levels of intensity through the summer, wintertime is when you need to start digging those foundations. It's widely misunderstood that endurance relates only to the ability to ride for multiple hours in the saddle. Not so – riding anaerobically can only be sustained for about one minute. All levels beneath the pain and power of an anaerobic effort take place aerobically and are considered to be endurance-based riding.

At its lowest intensity level, endurance riding can involve riding along at minimal intensities for hours at a time. Higher up the scale, when Type 2a muscle fibres are increasingly recruited on top of Type 1, an endurance effort would equate to a short-distance time trial, a circuit or an off-road race up to one hour. Pretty much the shortest endurance event, and one of the hardest, would be a pursuit race on the track, no further than 4km and lasting under five minutes.

The benefits of endurance training are:

- Improves the aerobic system – the heart and blood vessels grow and multiply.
- Muscle fibres grow mitochondria and become more efficient at converting chemical energy.
- 'Lean burn' muscles become better at using oxygen and use less stored glycogen at all intensities of riding.
- The body learns to burn fat alongside glycogen, pushing out glycogen depletion times from 90 minutes to two hours.
- Builds strength in the joints, tendons and ligaments – essential for withstanding intervals and power training later.
- Acclimatises the body to spending time in the saddle and refines pedalling technique – makes your cycling more efficient and economic.
- Long rides alone or in a group are very enjoyable, in winter just as much as in summer.

Endurance training **does not**:

- improve VO$_2$max as effectively as faster and/or harder efforts;
- increase maximal aerobic capacity;
- prepare you for short, hard efforts at threshold levels;
- turn you into a sprinter, breakaway specialist or faster rider.

Enjoy it!

Before drawing up your base training winter programme it's important to take into account not only how much time you can devote to endurance riding, but also the duration of the rides compared to your target events in the coming season. If your primary aim is to go flat out for one hour, you may only need to build endurance with rides up to two hours. If you are training for a major European sportive, duration eight hours, it would be wise in the build-up to do at least one endurance training ride of similar duration, as well as multiple rides of at least three hours.

Not without reason, endurance training is seen by many as the most pleasurable aspect of riding. It was why most of us got into cycling in the first place. Pedalling in a small friendly group along a country lane on a Sunday, with the whole day ahead of you, is one of the great joys of cycling. But as work and family life inevitably begin to crowd in, spending hours on the bike can become a rare treat. It's still a lot of fun, but fitting in even one long ride each week can become a stressful business.

> **FIT MYTH**
>
> Riding slowly for hours on end is ideal preparation for road racing.

It is important to know why you are riding an endurance session and whether it is the right duration for you. Duration should be measured in time, not distance, as conditions in winter can make a relatively short ride in mucky weather take a lot longer and be just as hard as a ride twice as long in summer. It might work for a few gifted professional riders who can handle massive workloads, recover quickly and throw in efforts of varying intensity after several hours. Most hobby cyclists, even serious ones, cannot find the time for long rides mixed with recovery to follow a pro schedule without succumbing to overtraining, illness and injury.

Winter months one and two: Slow build-up
Choose your own cross-training routine in this programme. Consider weight training for two of the sessions per week if you want to improve your sprint or if you are over 40. Any of these sessions can be replaced by a turbo ride, a run or other form of exercise if the weather is too bad. Cut the duration, though, if you are riding the turbo: one hour at constant level 2–3 is better than trying to do two hours with less effort.

Winter months three and four: Building speed
Again, replace a road session with a turbo one as above. Reduce running and seriously consider some weight training in the cross-training sessions. If training is going well, increase the duration of any of these sessions but cut back if you feel tired. Add a ride on Wednesday, when there is only a cross-training session, if you feel on top of things.

TABLE 5.1: WINTER ENDURANCE TRAINING PROGRAMME: MONTHS ONE AND TWO

Week	Monday	Tuesday	Wednesday	
1	Rest, recovery ride (level 1) or cross training	Ride @ level 2 for 60 min on a flat route	Cross training	
2	Rest, recovery ride or cross training	Ride @ level 2–3 for 60 min on a rolling route, level 3 uphill	Cross training	
3	Rest, recovery ride or cross training	Ride @ level 2 for 70 min on a rolling route, level 3 uphill	Cross training	
4	Ride @ level 1 for 40 min on a flat route	Rest	Ride @ level 2–3 for 60 min on a flat route	
5	Rest, recovery ride or cross training	Ride @ level 2 for 70 min on a rolling route, level 3 uphill	Cross training	
6	Rest, recovery ride or cross training	Ride @ level 2–3 for 60 min on a hilly route, pushing almost to level 4 uphill	Cross training	
7	Rest, recovery ride or cross training	Ride @ level 2–3 for 60 min (midway ride 20 min @ level 1)	Cross training	
8	Ride @ level 1 for 40 min on a flat route	Rest	Ride @ level 2–3 for 60 min on a flat route	

Thursday	Friday	Saturday	Sunday
Ride @ level 2 for 75 min on a flat route (middle 15 min @ solid level 3)	Rest, recovery ride or cross training	Ride @ level 2–3 for 60 min on a rolling route, level 4 uphill	Ride @ level 2 for 90 min on a flat route
Ride @ level 2 for 60 min on a flat route (middle 15 min @ solid level 3)	Rest, recovery ride or cross training	Ride @ level 2 for 40 min on a flat route (midway do 3 x 15 sec flat-out sprints, with 5 min level 2 between efforts)	Ride @ level 2 for 105 min on a flat route
Ride @ level 2 for 60 min on a flat route (midway ride 2 x 10 min @ level 3, with 5 min level 1 between sets)	Rest, recovery ride or cross training	Ride @ level 2–3 for 60 min on a flat route	Ride @ level 2 for 120 min on a rolling route
Rest	Ride @ level 2 and into 3 for 10–15 min, then ride a time trial on test circuit. Finish with 10 min @ level 1. (Or whatever you decide on as your fitness test)	Rest	Ride @ level 2–3 for 120 min on a rolling route
Ride @ level 2 for 60 min on a flat route (midway ride 2 x 10 min @ level 3, with 5 min level 1 between sets)	Rest, recovery ride or cross training	Ride @ level 2–3 for 60 min on a flat route	Ride @ level 2–3 for 120 min on a rolling route
Ride @ level 2 for 75 min on a rolling route	Rest, recovery ride or cross training	Ride @ level 2–3 for 60 min on a flat route	Ride @ level 2 for 105 min on a rolling route, with some sprints thrown in
Ride @ level 2 for 60 min on a hilly route (midway ride 2 x 3 min hill repeats @ level 3–4, with 3 min level 1 between sets)	Rest, recovery ride or cross training	Ride @ level 2 for 40 min on a flat route (midway do 3 x 15 sec sprints, with 5 min level 2 between efforts)	Ride @ level 2–3 for 120 min on a rolling route
Rest	Ride @ level 2 and into 3 for 15 min, then ride a time trial on test circuit. Finish with 10min @ level 1. (Or whatever you decide on as your fitness test)	Rest	Ride @ level 2–3 for 120 min on a rolling route

TABLE 5.2: WINTER ENDURANCE TRAINING PROGRAMME: MONTHS THREE AND FOUR

Week	Monday	Tuesday	Wednesday	
9	Rest or recovery ride	Ride @ level 2–3 for 60 min on a flat route with lots of corners. Practise good cornering technique and accelerations	Cross training	
10	Rest	Ride @ level 2 for 60 min on a rolling route (midway ride 20 min @ level 3)	Cross training	
11	Rest	Ride @ level 2–3 for 60 min on a rolling route, level 4 on hills.	Cross training	
12	Ride @ level 2–3 for 50 min on a rolling route	Rest	Ride @ level 2–3 for 60 min on a flat route	
13	Ride @ level 2 for 60 min on a rolling route (midway ride 2 x 15 min @ level 3, with 5 min level 1 between sets)	Cross training	Ride @ level 2–3 for 60 min on a flat route (midway ride 3 x 3 min @ level 4, with 3 min level 1 between sets)	
14	Recovery ride	Ride @ level 2 for 60 min on a rolling route (midway ride 20 min @ level 3)	Recovery ride and cross training, but reduce emphasis on weights now. However, try to do one heavy weights session every two weeks until the end of the season	
15	Rest	Ride @ level 2–3 for 60 min on a flat route (midway ride 4 x 3 min @ level 4 with 3 min level 1 between sets)	Rest	
16	Ride @ level 2–3 for 50 min on a rolling route	Rest	Ride @ level 2–3 for 60 min on a rolling route	

Thursday	Friday	Saturday	Sunday
Ride @ level 2 for 60 min on a rolling route (midway ride 2 x 10 min @ level 3 with 5 min level 1 between sets)	Rest, recovery ride or cross training	Ride @ level 2 for 60 min on a flat route (midway do 4 x 30 sec seated fast pedalling, with 2 min level 1 between efforts)	Ride @ level 2–3 for 70 min on a rolling route
Ride @ level 2 for 60 min on a rolling route (midway ride 3 x 5 min @ level 3–4 and last min @ level 4 with 5 min level 1 between sets)	Rest	Ride @ level 2 for 60 min on a flat route (midway do 3 x 15 sec sprints, with 5 min level 1 between efforts)	Ride @ level 2–4 for 70 min on a rolling multi-lap route. Practise cornering and accelerating hard out of corners. Sprint each lap
Ride @ level 2 for 60+ min on a rolling route (midway ride 4 x 5 min @ level 3–4 and last min @ level 4 with 5 min level 1 between sets)	Rest	Ride @ level 2–3 for 60+ min on a flat route (mid-way ride 3 x 5 min paceline @ level 3–4 with 5 min at level 1 between sets)	Ride @ level 2–3 for 80 min on a flat route
Rest	Ride @ level 2–3 for 15 min, then ride a time trial on test circuit. Finish with 10 min @ level 1	Rest	Rest or ride @ level 3 for 40 min on a flat route
Easy ride and/or cross training	Ride @ level 3 for 50 min on flat route (midway ride 4 x 30 sec seated, in high gear, with 2 min level 4 between efforts)	Easy ride or cross training	Ride @ level 2–3 for 70 min on a rolling route, level 4 uphill
Ride @ level 2 for 60 min on a rolling route (midway ride 4 x 5 min @ level 3–4, pushing to level 4 in last min, with 5 min level 1 between sets)	Rest	Ride @ level 2 for 60 min on a flat route (midway ride 4 x 5 min paceline @ level 3–4, with 5 min between sets)	Ride @ level 2–3 for 80 min on a rolling route, level 4 for last bit of every uphill
Ride @ level 2–3 for 60 min on hilly route, level 3–4 uphill. Sprint over the top of each hill into level 5	Rest	Ride @ level 2 for 40 min on flat route (midway do 3 x 30 sec seated fast pedalling, with 2 min level 1 between efforts)	Ride @ level 2–3 for 90 min on a rolling route, level 4 uphill
Recovery ride	Ride @ level 2–3 for 15 min, then ride a time trial on test circuit. Finish with 10 min @ level 1	Recovery ride	Rest or ride @ level 2–3 for 60 min on a flat route

Commuting – endurance for free

If you have the opportunity to use your bike to get to work, or have an excuse to cycle somewhere regularly, a couple of hours each day in the saddle can be an endurance godsend. If it's a ride through town then chances are that the safest way to ride is at a pace between recovery and brisk. Short hills, traffic lights and quieter roads beyond the town centre can also be used for fartlek intervals – randomly spaced hard threshold efforts of varying length – which will help spice up your ride and maintain some top end.

You could also incorporate longer, up to 20-minute, blocks of brisk effort when road conditions allow. You need to feel fresh and it's not worth pushing yourself after a tough day at work, but this is another way of training Type 1 endurance muscle fibres with increasing amounts of Type 2a. Into the new year and as the nights begin to draw out, the potential for a longer ride home is increasingly attractive. A ten-mile loop into the countryside can also be used to get clear of the traffic and up the tempo.

TABLE 5.3: TWO-HOUR DAILY COMMUTING PLAN		
	To	**From**
Monday	Day off/recovery	Day off/recovery
Tuesday	20 min brisk	20 min brisk
Wednesday	Steady	Steady
Thursday	20 min brisk	Fartlek
Friday	Steady	Steady

FOCUS ON

Progression

Hard exercise, or at least harder than you are used to, causes damage to your muscles, and stresses your cardiovascular system and metabolic pathways. In response to this stress and damage, your body repairs itself when you rest, but it reinforces the repair in response to the exercise that has caused the damage. So next time you exercise you will be better able to cope with the same level of stress. To improve further you now need to exercise harder to cause more breakdown, and in due course stronger repair. That is why any training schedule must get progressively harder.

There are two things to consider in the progressive overload process. You must factor in rest to give the repairs time to take hold, and you must eat a balanced diet (see chapter 7), including lots of protein, to give your body the raw materials to repair. Also, you cannot hurry this exercise–repair response by going over the top and doing a lot of training at once. It has to be done in measured steps to allow your body to keep pace. You will only make big leaps in fitness by making the journey in baby steps.

RIDER STORY

Dan Fleeman is a professional cyclist on the GB and continental scene.

'I really listen to my body when I train, and I've found that I make the biggest leaps in fitness when I combine training a little below my anaerobic threshold (mid to high Level 3, brisk) with training at close to my VO$_2$max. You have to be very precise to train like this, but if you do it right you can do more work using this method than you can by doing the classic time trial or threshold intervals that most riders use.

'First find out what your anaerobic threshold is. You need to know what it means in terms of heart rate or power output. When you know that, you can do what I call sweet-spot intervals.

'To do these you ride at about five beats below your threshold heart rate, so you are going hard but not red-lining it. When you do that you can do quite long intervals – 10, 15 or 20 minutes – during which you are pushing up your threshold from below but you aren't building lots of fatigue or lactate in your muscles.

'You end up being able to do longer intervals with less damage than if you work on your threshold, but you still get the threshold training effect. In fact because the intervals are longer you get more.

'Now, if you get a good base of these long intervals in, building up the duration of them all the time, you can add VO$_2$max intervals on other days. For these I go as hard as I can for three minutes, simple as that.

'A good plan is to have a sweet-spot day and an easy day, and then do some VO$_2$max intervals. I've raised my threshold by doing those two sessions and without once doing a real threshold session.

'The other thing to remember, though, is that you need to keep testing yourself, or getting tested to see what your threshold is. And when you get a new threshold figure you must change your training levels along with it.'

Love winter!

Many cyclists approach the off season with a sense of gloom and foreboding. As the road season draws to a close and long rides are curtailed by shorter days and deteriorating weather, it's natural to feel despondent and even depressed. Cycling seriously can be an all-consuming lifestyle. If you compete regularly, it's a sport with terrific highs and character-building lows. Coming to the end of a busy summer and autumn of riding and racing can lead to a sense of loss, even bereavement. It is wise to recognise the signs and either have systems in place that can get you through the low times, or seek professional help.

The good news is that most cyclists take a positive view of life and many will welcome the chance to have a rest, try a new fitness regime or even race in a new cycling discipline during the four- or five-month winter season. Taking a well-earned break, a holiday in October or November for instance, is a great way to mark the end of the summer season and the start of the winter programme. Gone are the days when the only exercise a cyclist took before January was digging up the potatoes for Christmas dinner. These days a break of two or three weeks is plenty and will probably have you chomping at the bit to burn off some energy at the end of it. Keep the break inside a month and it will not be hard to return to a level of fitness that will enable you to tackle a range of activities.

Starting a non-cycling activity, however, demands a cautious approach as there will be new techniques to learn and muscles to pull! In this chapter we recommend non-cycling fitness activities which include gym work and cross training. Then there are sports which in some ways mimic cycling that can be excellent for maintaining leg power. Finally, bike racing in winter has never been more popular and ranges from indoor on tracks to off-road and road racing on closed circuits.

Cross training

Finding a cross-discipline sport which complements your cycling and can be squeezed in during busy periods, or when you cannot get out due to bad weather, is well worth pursuing. A different activity during the off season is also a great way to take a break from bike riding, especially if you have just come to the end of a long cycling season.

More importantly, cross training is good for building upper-body and core strength, lost after a summer of cycling. A game-based activity is also good for co-ordination and reaction times, both of which are worth honing in the off season. Anything that gets you running is also great for your breathing, heart and lungs.

Skiing, especially cross-country, and speed skating – the sister sport of cycling – are two more cycling-specific and exciting sports to consider. Working out in a gym, from weight training to spinning classes, and running are popular options for wintering cyclists. Training with weights is a winter activity that many cyclists swear by. It's not for everyone, however, and there are those who argue against it. For older cyclists and riders looking to make real gains in power (for track racing for instance), weights are an all-year-round discipline.

Gym workouts

For busy cyclists and riders who have to endure hard winters, membership of a gym can be a godsend. Gym training is also an efficient way to address any weaknesses you might have, especially in your core, upper body and back. A gym workout is even more attractive if you work in an office and can sneak in an extra training session during your lunch break. That could involve using weight machines for upper body and legs, a rowing machine or a skiing simulator. You can also run on the treadmill or ride a static bicycle. Useful classes include spinning for leg speed and aerobic fitness, and Pilates for core strength.

For older cyclists, gym workouts with strength and flexibility exercises offer the opportunity to target age-related niggles and old injuries. The inevitable decline in muscle-mass and fast-twitch Type 2b muscle fibres can also be significantly reduced by training with weights.

Gym work for

- Core strength
- Muscular power
- Increasing aerobic fitness

Equipment
Depends on the gym, but most will have weight machines, treadmills, free weights, spinning machines, rowing machines and core strength exercisers such as Swiss balls.

Downside
Too many upper-body workouts can add muscle that will not help you on the bike, especially on the climbs. Apart from track sprinters, you need to concentrate more on core strength than on bulk-building arm and shoulder exercises.

Running

Running suits anyone with less than an hour to spare, those who can only get out at night during winter, or cyclists just looking for an alternative and fun workout in the fresh air. That is the conventional wisdom and it still holds true; but there's more to it than that, as recent research has shown that running can make you a better cyclist and is worth incorporating into your annual schedule.

As a calorie burning exercise, running beats cycling hands down if you are looking to lose a few kilograms or just maintain your end-of-season weight through the winter. An hour of running burns 300 more calories than an hour of cycling, if both are performed at the same level of effort or heart rate. Running is great for cardiovascular fitness and general athleticism. It gets you out of your bike-riding crouch and exercises the back, core, shoulder and arm muscles in a way that translates well to cycling.

The impact nature of running can also benefit cyclists, as it helps to strengthen bones and ligaments in the legs, knees, ankles, hips and back. Reduced bone density has been identified in young cyclists and this can lead to osteopenia (lower than normal bone density) and osteoporosis (very low bone density).

Start slow and short

Going from a non-load bearing activity, like cycling, to an impact sport, like running, is often where cyclists go wrong. A fit cyclist will not run out of breath at the end of the road and strong legs will not tire easily either. But the shock of running after a season on the bike can cause muscular pain and even joint injury if it's not approached in bite-size sessions. Start with a 10-minute run, and up the distance by no more than 5 per cent from week to week.

Running may not exercise the quad muscles like cycling does, and cycling is less reliant on muscles used in running, such as the calves, glutes and ankles. But running does them no harm, and if you can run off-road, and especially up hills, this type of workout will strengthen muscles and ligaments in the lower leg and give your quads a good workout too.

Running for

- Stronger, more dense bones and ligaments
- Stronger core
- Exercising arms and shoulders
- Improving cardiovascular fitness – best for increasing VO_2max
- Burning calories faster than cycling

Equipment

Running's trump card is that it's cheap to get into (compared to cycling) and portable, and it is perfect for the time-hungry cyclist. All you need is a pair of running shoes, running shorts and a vest. It's worth making sure the shoes are suited to your gait, and most specialist running shops will give you advice based on a treadmill test machine. Try on shoes that are half to one size bigger than your normal shoe size. Running shorts are lightweight and won't chafe, and in winter it's also worth wearing a pair of running or compression tights. If you intend to run off-road it's also worth buying a pair of trail or cross-country shoes with grippy soles and a more robust upper.

Downside

There is a risk of muscle strain and injury from running if you launch into long, hard runs after lots of time on the bike. Start off slow and short, working up from 10 minutes in 5 per cent increments, twice a week. Only when you can do 30 minutes with no aches and pains should you consider longer runs of up to 45 minutes or one hour.

Skiing and skating

Alpine skiing is a good workout, though more for leg power than aerobic fitness. Downhill slalom, carving aggressively down a slope, works the glutes and quads in a very similar way to cycling. If you are lucky enough to have regular access to a ski slope you will notice the benefit as soon as you get back into the saddle.

Cross-country skiing and skating are great endurance workouts in a style that uses the same muscles as cycling. Traditional cross-country skiing uses tracks in the snow at ski resorts around the world. As a holiday with some hard exercise thrown in, cross-country skiing is hard to beat. In fact if you do a lot of it you need to make sure you do not overtrain and arrive at the start of the following season too fit!

In-line skating matches cross-country skiing but can be done in the dry, in parks and along metalled tracks. It's much easier to get the hang of than cross-country skiing and is more accessible to city dwellers. Once again, you can overdo it, and it's worth mixing endurance with some speed work to mimic your own cycling targets.

Skiing and skating for

- Building aerobic endurance
- Increasing leg power
- Training similar muscles to cycling

Equipment

Skis for alpine and cross-country skiing, as well as thermal and safety gear, are not cheap to buy. It is best to hire the equipment if you are on holiday. In-line skates cost about the same as a good pair of cycling shoes and can be worn with cycling gear, with knee pads over cycling tights.

Downside

Accessibility to snowfields makes skiing little more than a holiday activity for many. There is also a significant risk of injury, especially for alpine skiers. Learning the basics and developing skills on skis takes time and money.

Weight training

Weight training has gone in and out of fashion in the cycling world, although it has always had its adherents, and most authorities agree now that they were right. The weights room features large in the programmes of most pro racers, and not just in the winter. Many top pros go back to the weights at specific times during the year to reinforce the gains they made in winter.

However, a word of caution: training with weights requires perfect technique, and it isn't a contest to see how much you can lift. In fact doing an exercise with perfect form will bring better results than concentrating on how much you can lift. The reason for this is that, although weight training builds strength by working your muscles hard, it also builds specific core strength, but only when every exercise is done to the letter.

The following exercises are the best ones to support and improve your cycling, but you need to get some qualified instruction on how to do them correctly.

For free weights you need to know

· Deadlift

· Front squat

· Back squat

· Bench press

- Bent-over row

For weights machines you need to use

- Leg press
- Bench press
- Seated row

However, machines do not train your core as well as free weights. You could always ask the instructor to evaluate your posture and recommend other exercises, but the ones given above, along with a full core workout at the end of the session (see page 000), should be the heart of your weight training.

Weight training for

- Leg strength
- Explosive power
- Upper body stability
- Back strength
- Bone and tendon strength

Cyclist's weights programme

- Warm up with any cardio exercise that involves using the whole body.
- Perform three sets of dead-lifts, front or back squats, bench presses and bent rows.
- Do a full core session, including work with a Swiss ball.
- Start your programme at the beginning of winter by doing 12 repetitions (reps) of each weight exercise.
- Progress by increasing the weight when you can do 12 reps with perfect form. Then, while keeping perfect form, begin to reduce the number of reps as you increase the weight. Eventually you should aim to do five sets of 5 to 8 reps of each exercise with a heavy weight to build real cycling power.
- Reduce the number of sessions towards the end of winter, but still try to do one heavy session of weights every two weeks throughout the season. Keep on with your core work at least two or three times a week for the whole year.

Core training

Sit on the ball and walk forwards, rolling the ball up your back. Raise your hips until your torso is level with the floor. Support the shoulders, neck and head on the ball, keeping the torso flat and parallel to the ground with the knees bent at right angles and feet hip-width apart, flat on the floor. Rest hands lightly on hips. Hold for one minute and repeat three times.

To add a balancing element to the previous exercise, lift one leg at a time and hold for 30 seconds. Keep the leg in line with the rest of your body, parallel to the ground. Repeat on the other side for five sets.

Position yourself with the ball under your thighs and hands on the floor. Keeping your back straight, slightly bend your elbows and hold for one minute. Repeat three times.

To add press-ups walk forwards on your arms until just the feet and shins are resting on the ball. Keep your back and legs and neck in a straight line. Try not to lower your head or lift your behind. Lower your chest towards the ground. Slowly push back to the starting position and repeat 10 times, working up to sets of three.

This is an alternative to sit-ups and crunches. Sit on top of the ball with your back straight and hands lightly on hips. Using the legs and core to maintain shape and balance, walk forwards a few small steps holding your torso and shoulders in line. Repeat 10 times and work up to sets of three.

Stretching

Stretching is an important part of injury prevention and recovery. It's also relaxing, promotes circulation and increases the range of motion, which is good for you and great for adopting a more aero position on the bike. There are many stretches that you can perform and most athletes will pick up on a few that are most relevant to them. That can be the best way to perfect a stretch and ensure that you do it regularly.

Hamstrings

Sit on the floor and lean forwards from the hips, reaching down one leg towards your foot while supporting your upper body. Try to keep the back as flat as possible, hold the stretch for up to 60 seconds then slowly release and swap legs. Feel the stretch in the rear of the upper part of the leg, especially behind the knee.

Don't do the classic touching your toes with a bent spine, bouncing up and down, trying to get lower. This is bad for your spine, and the pivot is on your hips, rather than stressing the legs.

Quads

Cyclists with big quads can struggle to get a good stretch with the usual standing-up method, pulling the opposite leg up to the buttocks. To get a bigger stretch sit with your legs bent under you and support your body weight on your hands, feeding in the stretch by leaning back. Hold for 20 seconds before repeating. Keep the back straight and be very careful with this stretch if you have knee issues. Avoid doing it on hard ground.

Calves

Calf muscles get very tight from cycling and this stretch is good for relieving tired muscles. Make like you are pushing down a wall, with your weight on the bent leading leg. Feel the stretch behind the knee and down the calf, and increase the stretch if you want by putting the leading leg further forward.

Abductors

This stretch is very important for firing and supporting the larger muscle groups in the tops of the legs. Sit upright and draw your feet towards your groin until you can feel a stretch. Then grab your ankles and brace your elbows against the knees, force the knees towards the ground and stretch the groin 'manually'. Hold for 30 seconds and repeat.

Glutes and lower back

This stretch is effective for the back and lower hip area and releases tension from the lower back. Bend one leg and place the foot of this leg over by the side of the opposite knee. Then trap the knee of the bent leg with the elbow of the opposite arm. Place the other arm directly behind your body and then turn your hips to allow you to look directly behind you.

Lower back and hip flexors

Tension in the lower back and hip flexors can be released by performing this cross-legged stretch. Lie flat on the ground and bend one leg. Then place the opposite ankle on top of the bent knee. Clasp your hands behind your upper leg and pull both legs towards your chest. You will feel the stretch in the hips and gluteus regions of the crossed-over leg. Hold for 20 seconds then change legs.

Lower back

This simple stretch is great for the lower back. Curl up in a ball and pull both knees towards the chest. Just do a small stretch each time and you will feel it in the gluteus, mid and lower back muscles. Hold for 30 seconds and repeat.

Arms

This stretch also relieves tension in the shoulders and back. Bend your elbow as if to scratch your opposite ear, behind your head. With the other hand, grasp the hand of the bent arm and pull it firmly but steadily down the back. You can feel the stretch down the triceps and shoulder muscles on the bent-arm side. Hold for 20 seconds and repeat for other arm.

Cyclo-cross and mountain biking

There has been a boom in cyclo-cross, especially in the USA, and it's no mystery why: it's a one-hour workout at an intensity that is virtually impossible to replicate in training. Cyclo-cross is also a superb test of bike handling skills; it takes place on the dirt, so when you fall off, it should not hurt too much, although it's a good idea to avoid trees and rocks.

It's a myth that cyclo-cross is a sport with lots of running (with the bike slung over one shoulder), broken up by fiddly technical riding with little physical benefit to the cyclist. These days there is hardly any running on cyclo-cross courses: the total time off the bike during a lap of between five and ten minutes can be counted in just a few seconds per lap. Unless you are training specifically for a race with lots of sandy sections or very muddy climbs, running need only play a small part in your training week.

As an anaerobic cycling workout, cyclo-cross is unrivalled in intensity and as a winter training activity, nothing comes close. Only the most ferocious turbo session can get near to the efforts made in a one-hour cross race. Racing around a circuit with a mix of terrain, a cross race is a series of short sprints, each one at full power, as hard as the rider can go, but only lasting between 5 and 25 seconds. Only the shortest bursts are at full power, but up to a third of a race can be anaerobic. Between the full-power efforts can be varying lengths of effort well below threshold when the rider is negotiating an obstacle, say a tricky downhill or a section through trees.

Then there is the start, crucial for race position, which demands around a minute of flat-out riding at up to 150 per cent of threshold. If you suffer from pre-race nerves, cyclo-cross is a great way to conquer them, every weekend throughout the winter.

Cyclo-cross workouts (Frank Overton, FasCat Coaching)

Interval training session

Allow at least one day to recover from this for a race on Sunday. It can be done on a flat piece of grass on a short circuit or on a turbo trainer.

- Ride 20 seconds flat out, 10 seconds easy between bursts
- Do this seven times then take four minutes' rest
- Repeat two or three times

These are Tabata intervals – very hard on full power with a short rest period that barely allows for recovery and makes the effort in the second and third sets very hard indeed, both physically and mentally.

Race start

You need a little off-road circuit for this with, if possible, room for a fast start then a short climb, a technical section, and a barrier or short climb requiring a dismount.

- Simulate a race start with one foot in the right pedal and your brain in 'attack' mode
- Push off, clip in and go very hard, at up to 150 per cent of threshold for one minute, negotiating the obstacles at race speed
- Ease off and ride another two laps at threshold pace
- Repeat three to five times

Motor-pacing

Not an easy one to organise but if you have a friend with a motorbike, scooter or moped, motor-pacing is a terrifically effective way to mirror the efforts made in a cyclo-cross event and there are few better ways to maintain speed. It's also a lot of fun, though hazardous, just like a real bike race. This is a workout that need not last longer than one hour and could even be just a 30-minute block at the end of a training ride, with an agreed meeting place for rider and motor-pacer, and a quiet stretch of road.

A road with short but not too steep climbs is best, as the extra effort you'll need to make to stay in contact when the motor-pacer goes uphill is similar to the demands on one cross rider trying to follow another. If there are a few turns don't worry, as the effort required to get back up to speed (anything from 25 to 30mph) is also very close to a short anaerobic acceleration in cyclo-cross. Just make sure that you have a good rapport with your motor-pacer, that both of you know the route and that all manoeuvres are executed smoothly and predictably.

All of the above workouts are hard and should only be done once a week, with rest or easy riding days either side. A cyclo-cross race may only last one hour, but it's such an intense workout that it's imperative to be rested before resuming a tough training session.

Cyclo-cross wheel tips

- Run tyres at much lower pressures than you would on the road. In slippery conditions you can have less than 40psi in wired-on tyres and under 30psi in tubulars.
- Tubular tyres make a big difference as they can be run at lower pressures than wired-on tyres and do not suffer from pinch flats. The rims are stronger and lighter too. Worth the extra trouble (gluing them on) and expense if you are serious about cross.
- Another set of wheels, possibly with a different choice of off-road tyre, is well worth having. A spare bike is even more useful, especially in muddy conditions when a helper can wash the muddy one after each bike change.

Mountain bike

If you do not have a cyclo-cross bike, a mountain bike can be used in a cyclo-cross race. While not ideal – they are generally heavier than cross bikes and harder to carry, and can feel a little slower – a mountain bike can still provide a tough workout with more sure-footed handling.

Alternatively, there are often mountain bike races in winter, on courses better suited to a mountain bike's capabilities. Longer flowing trails and climbs with little or no running are better suited to fat-tyred machines and the effort is more aerobic, especially if the race lasts longer than one hour.

Winter track riding

Training and racing on a track through the winter is another good way to maintain speed and enthusiasm. An indoor track is best but many open-air ones also have evening and weekend training sessions in which it is possible to ride in groups and even practise motor-pacing. Some of the bigger tracks also have winter leagues and headline events open to the public. Now that the UCI World Cup track series has moved to winter and the world championships to spring, the winter months are treated as the main track season.

It's well worth finding your local track as even the older outdoor ones with shallow bankings can be used for a safe training session and might even have an organised road bike group ride once a week. A floodlit outdoor track has obvious advantages over a night training ride on the open road.

Road racing

The increasing popularity of purpose-built road circuits closed to motor traffic has led to a steady growth in rides and races during the off season. Milder winters may have helped but a generally higher level of fitness among cyclists has ensured that winter race series on these circuits attract big fields. Expect a criterium-type workout at 25mph or more, lasting around one hour. There is no question that it's a good workout, but riders coming off a busy summer should be careful to avoid staleness from the travel and stresses of winter competition.

FOCUS ON

Variety and enjoyment in your training

Choose the activities you enjoy and go at them wholeheartedly, but don't do something just because you think you should be doing it. For example, weight training is good, but if you hate it don't do it. You probably run the risk of getting injured if you do anyway. Also, remember that you are a cyclist and as the winter progresses you'll need to cut out the variety to do more riding. If you discover you like doing another sport more, then do that instead.

And if you really love cycling so much that you resent time away from your bike, then by all means ride through the winter. You might miss some of the all-round strengthening that other activities can offer, but you'll be building a big base of specific exercise. Just don't batter yourself too hard too early on the bike. You need to save some enthusiasm and aggression for your targets in the summer.

It's nice to have a blowout in the winter, have a few drinks, eat things that you wouldn't normally eat. In fact it's a good thing to do that. However, one thing you can do to really help your performance is keep an eye on your weight. You don't need to get compulsive with the scales, just don't forget where they are. It's healthy to put a bit of weight on, but don't let it get out of hand because it will compromise your training. You don't want to be restricting what you eat in order to lose a lot of weight when you start your hard training.

RIDER STORY

Liam Killeen is a professional mountain biker and off-road racer and shows that it's possible to race all year round and make good progress, like other top mountain bikers, by combining his summer sport with cyclo-cross in the winter. Endurance track riders, especially those who do the winter six-day races, are often good summer road riders.

Killeen is Britain's best cross-country mountain bike racer, but most winters he makes an appearance in top cyclo-cross events, and regularly places in the national championships. This is how he does it.

'I take a break after the last mountain bike race of the year, a complete rest for two weeks, then slowly build back up through October and the first part of November, exactly as I would if I wasn't going to ride any cross and was just getting ready for the first mountain bike race the following spring.

'However, at the beginning of December I begin some intensive cyclo-cross work, and after three weeks I will have a try-out race. The nationals are the end of the first week of January, so I keep my intensive work going through Christmas, with maybe doing a couple of local cross races, and see what I can do in the nationals off that. After the race I back off a bit for a rest, then get back to my winter programme.

'The cross championships are like having a mini-peak in the middle of winter, and to be honest I think a month of speed work does me good, so long as I get straight back to distance training after it.

'I don't have to spend as long finding some speed for the first mountain bike race either. I think of my cyclo-cross racing as a nice little island in the middle of winter that keeps me buzzing.'

Fast fuel

In this chapter we will look at one of the most important components of an advanced training plan. No matter how much work you put in on the bike, the benefits will never be truly felt if you cannot fuel your training and recovery with a clear nutritional strategy. There is an adaptive response from the body to every type of session, from short-duration power workouts to endurance rides of an hour or more. Every physical effort you make requires fuel, not just for the exertion itself, but also to cope with the after-effects, when the body recovers, makes repairs and adapts to loads placed upon it.

Knowing how your everyday meals can benefit your cycling, as well as how to integrate supplementary fuels, like protein shakes, into your diet, will ensure that you are making the most of your training. Just like an engine, high-octane fuel in the tank and top quality oil in the sump both ensure optimum performance with minimal wear and tear.

How you plan your eating and drinking either side of when you are actually exercising is one of the essential building blocks of your overall condition. For the most part this is not just a nutritional strategy to make you a better cyclist; it's the basis for a healthy balanced diet which will contribute to your wellbeing whatever your circumstances. This means that, occasional treat apart, you should strive to maintain the principles of healthy eating even during periods of time away from the bike, either during the winter or through illness and injury, and especially on rest days.

Changing your diet, cutting out bad habits and learning new recipes can take time and you should not expect to make big changes overnight. This is a long-term shift in your lifestyle which will be easier to sustain if you take your time and do things at a comfortable pace. If you are also trying to lose weight and keep it off, a long-term strategy is by far the best solution.

In contrast, eating and drinking while on the bike is something that you can address and make changes to with instant results. There is a bewildering choice of energy drinks, gels and snack bars in the sports nutrition market. Cycling-specific products have been developed for before, during and after riding, and knowing which ingredients to look for will greatly help you to make the correct choice of product. Sports energy products can be expensive, so we will also suggest natural alternatives, wherever possible, for budget-conscious riders.

Everyday eating

Just to function normally it is necessary to consume between 1900kcal (women) and 2500kcal (men) each day. It would be easy to hit those energy figures with cheeseburgers and fries, but for a serious cyclist the imbalance of nutrients would undo much of the good work put in through riding. The key to everyday eating is to maintain a balance between macronutrients, micronutrients and water. Listed below are the food components which make up both categories and the third component, water. Energy figures in kilocalories per gram are given for the macronutrients.

Carbohydrate should form the majority of your diet, especially if your training is endurance-led. Around 60 per cent of a cyclist's daily intake should be carbohydrate-based, with protein at 18 per cent (more if the training is in a muscle building or power phase) and 22 per cent made up of healthy fats.

MACRONUTRIENTS	MICRONUTRIENTS	HYDRATION
Carbohydrate – 4kcal/g	Vitamins	Water
Fat – 9kcal/g	Minerals	
Protein – 4kcal/g		
Alcohol – 7kcal/g		

Carbohydrate

Carbohydrate is the body's number one source of energy and should account for around 60–70 per cent of your daily calorific intake. Compared to protein and fat, carbohydrate converts to energy – stored as glycogen in the muscles – faster and more comprehensively, providing power for daily physical activity, as well as blood glucose for brain function and the central nervous system.

When there is a supply of carbohydrate it spares protein in the body from breaking down into glucose. Protein can then continue doing its primary job of growth and repair. Fat burning is also more complete and efficient in the presence of adequate stores of carbohydrate. If carbohydrate is in short supply fat breakdown is less efficient and can result in excessive amounts of ketones (partly broken-down fats), leading to tiredness, nausea and loss of appetite.

Carbohydrate is stored as glycogen in the muscles, blood and liver and while there may be enough for a day of sedentary activity, cycling carbohydrate stores can go from full to empty in about 90 minutes. There can be few cyclists who have not experienced that light-headed feeling and hollow stomach that signal the final drain-ing of the body's store of carbohydrate. Hunger knock, or the 'bonk', is best avoided by carrying carb drinks and foods or gel with you on the bike.

Glycaemic index (GI)

Not all carbohydrates are equal. Carbohydrate-rich foodstuffs break down into simple sugars at differing rates and knowing where each type sits in the glycaemic index is key to maintaining a predominantly high-fibre, complex-carb diet best suited to cycling. There is a place for carbohydrates from opposite ends of the GI, ranging from fast release high-GI foodstuffs for competition and rapid recovery, to slow release low-GI for post-training recovery and repair.

GLYCAEMIC INDEX

How quickly different sources of carbohydrate are absorbed can be ascertained from the Glycaemic Index of each carb type. Quickly absorbed carbohydrates, like bananas, chocolate and rice cakes, are ideal for a rapid energy boost. These have a high GI number and are suitable for energy during and immediately before and after exercise. Low GI carbs include pulses and oats and are suitable for a slow-burn energy release when eaten a few hours before exercise.

GI CLASSIFICATION

Low: 55 or below

Medium: 56–69

High: 70 or above

Low GI foodstuffs	Medium GI foodstuffs	High GI foodstuffs
Unsweetened muesli (40)	Porridge (58)	Weetabix (74)
Wholemeal bread (49)	Croissant (67)	Baguette (95)
Broccoli (10)	Couscous (61)	Bagel (72)
Brown rice (50)	Baked potato (60)	Scone (92)
Pearl barley (22)	Banana (58)	White rice (86)
Spaghetti (32)	Raisins (64)	Mashed potato (73)
Red lentils (21)		Chips (75)
Butter beans (36)		Dates (103)

Fat

Fat is not the great evil that it is made out to be in some quarters. If your only goal is to lose weight and you are not an athlete, fat is high on the list of foodstuffs to avoid. But as an active and hopefully not too overweight cyclist, you can take a more balanced and intelligent approach to fat. Primarily fat is a dense form of energy. Compared to carbohydrate it contains twice the energy (nine kilocalories per gram compared to four). Carbohydrate remains the preferred source, however, because fat releases its energy more slowly and it slows the digestion.

Fat can be stored (in adipose cells) in much higher quantities than carbohydrate and is the largest and most efficient energy source in the body. It metabolises fat-soluble vitamins A, D, E and K, protects vital body organs, lubricates body tissue and insulates the body. An athlete can healthily consume 15 to 30 per cent fat.

Saturated fats, which are often referred to as 'bad fats' and are solid at room temperature, should be avoided as they are linked to high cholesterol and heart disease. Bad fats are found in meat, cheese, cakes and biscuits. Saturated and trans fats or hydrogenated fats should be avoided as they are associated with a build-up of unhealthy cholesterol.

Good fats

These fats, normally liquid at room temperature (such as olive oil), are good for you in many ways. Primarily, though, they lower cholesterol, act as fuel and reduce inflammation, which is especially useful for athletes in training. Good fats do other things too, such as reduce the risk of heart attacks and strokes.

The only thing a cyclist in training needs to remember is that there are two types of these fatty acids: omega 3 and omega 6. There are many dietary sources of these, but think oily fish, like tuna and mackerel, and fish oils for omega 3, and seeds for omega 6. You need both omega fatty acids in your diet, and supplements aren't a bad way of getting them.

Protcin

Protein is not a great source of energy, and it only kicks in when carbohydrates and fat stores are both running low. At an extreme level the body breaks down muscle protein for energy and this can lead to loss of muscle mass, especially in a long and arduous endurance event. Protein is essential for the creation of muscle, new bone and skin and a cyclist in training needs to consume more than the 0.8 grams per kilogram of body weight recommended for a sedentary person.

A cyclist's diet should comprise 15 to 20 per cent protein, depending on how hard you are training. Surplus protein is excreted through urea but can put excessive strain on the kidneys. Increasing fluid intake is recommended if you are taking in extra protein. Regular training has been shown to accelerate the breakdown of protein, which is hardly surprising when muscles are suffering from micro-damage with each hard session. If there are insufficient reserves of carbohydrate, however, protein breakdown can be doubled and that makes it imperative for cyclists in hard training to increase daily carbohydrate intake up to 75 per cent.

A cyclist in heavy training needs 1.7 to 2 grams of protein per kilogram of body weight. That is a lot, though, and it's only recommended during very heavy training. One other aspect of protein is that when eaten with carbohydrates it slows down the rate at which the carbs are processed by your body, resulting in a slower release of energy than if that carb foodstuff was eaten on its own. Basically, all carbohydrates have their glycaemic index lowered when combined with protein.

Protein foods
Eggs
Fish
Lean meat
Beans, lentils, pulses
Yoghurt, cheese, milk
Nuts

Alcohol

High in calories and low on its usefulness to an athlete, alcohol is stored almost immediately as fat and as a result it can take longer to burn off than stores of carbohydrate. Drinking alcohol during an event is a mistake, as it can impair reaction times and co-ordination as well as temperature regulation. Alcohol is a diuretic – drink it after an event and it will not help you to rehydrate nearly as well as water, so make sure you take water or a recovery drink as well as your post-ride beer.

If you like an alcoholic drink after a ride, and we are all human, console yourself with this fact. Your body is acidic after a tough workout and beer actually helps push it towards neutral, which is the ideal mark. Don't drink too many, though, or the after-effects undo the good of all those miles you did. Also wine, although acidic, helps you digest meat, and red wine has a lot of anti-oxidants, which mitigate the damage exercise does to you. So a glass or two of wine with your evening meal will do you more good than harm. Just like for beer, make sure you are well hydrated before you drink wine.

Vitamins and minerals

These micronutrients are vital to the body's function, including cell metabolism and generation – they help wounds heal up and fortify the immune system. They also fight infection, send nerve impulses, help blood coagulate, control fluid balance and do many more small but vital jobs. A balanced diet should provide enough vitamins and minerals, but the only way to tell if you are deficient in a specific element is to have a blood test.

Vitamins A, D, E and K are soluble in fat. Vitamins B and C are soluble in water. Water-soluble vitamins need to be replenished every day, because they are not retained very well by the body. Fat is processed more slowly and will retain vitamins for longer, but it's important not to completely exclude good fats from your diet. The good news is that all of them are found in fruit, vegetables and everyday food like meat, fish, dairy produce and eggs. Fruit and vegetables should be as fresh as possible and the five-a-day guidelines for fruit and veg should be your start; get more down you if possible. Go for strongly coloured vegetables and a mixture of textures and you should comfortably achieve your body's vitamin requirements.

Minerals essential to the cyclist are calcium, iron and zinc. Calcium is essential for building and maintaining strong bones and can be taken from dairy products. Iron helps transport oxygen in the blood and is found in liver, beans, nuts and dried fruit. A lack of iron can result in a debilitating lack of energy and should not be confused with overtraining. Zinc helps to break down and use carbohydrate as well as synthesise protein. It bolsters the immune system and is very important in building muscle. Zinc is found in shellfish, meat, bread and cheese. Extra zinc becomes important as you age, particularly for men.

Water

It is widely understood that adequate hydration is a base-level requirement in everyday life and in sports. In recent years the bottle of water in one hand has become almost as ubiquitous as a mobile phone! Many people have become so accustomed to loading up with the recommended two or more litres of water a day (some of which can come from food) that there have been warnings of the dangers of hyponatraemia – or water intoxication – which is when excessive water dilutes the blood. Blood sodium levels can drop to dangerously low levels in this state, but it can be avoided or managed by drinking electrolyte fluids and eating salty foods.

Cyclists need to be particularly mindful of dehydration as they can find themselves working hard for long periods of time and in all weather conditions. When you consider that water constitutes up to 65 per cent of a male's body weight and 55 per cent of a female's, the effects of dehydration on performance are clear. Deprive yourself of water for a week and you can die.

Fluid is lost through sweating, excretion, breathing and the skin. In hot weather, fluid replacement can run at one litre per hour (two cycling bottles), double the normal amount required in normal or cold conditions. It's important to maintain hydration at these levels even if it feels like you may not be sweating, in winter for instance. It's too late to start drinking only when you feel the effects of thirst – always take a bottle on every ride and aim to finish it before you get home. Even low levels of dehydration can lead to a double-digit drop in performance.

Hydration

- Regulates body temperature
- Helps transport nutrients and clear waste products from them
- Gives shape to cells
- Helps form structure of glycogen and protein molecules
- Refreshes mucus secretions and joint fluids
- Provides a medium for chemical reactions
- Produces light-coloured urine

Dehydration

- Decreases sweat rate
- Decreases heat dissipation
- Increases body core temperature
- Reduces blood volume
- Increases rate of muscle glycogen usage
- Decreases skin blood flow
- Causes dry mouth and headache
- Provokes muscle cramps and gastric distress
- Reduces immune system defences
- Leads to a risk of heat stroke and organ failure
- Results in death if fluid losses are from 12 to 15 per cent
- Produces dark-coloured urine

TIP

Drink water on training, race and rest days. It is essential to stay hydrated all of the time as it helps your body to work optimally.

Fluid types

Fluid enters the body through the stomach, and different types of liquid empty at varying rates.

- Isotonic: Formulated to be in balance with the body's fluids. Isotonic drinks typically contain 5 to 8 per cent carbohydrate, with sodium added to aid absorption. They are suitable for drinking at any time as they will not hinder hydration (e.g. Lucozade Sport, Isostar, Gatorade)

- Hypotonic: Empty faster from the gut than anything else and have low levels of carbohydrates and minerals. Easy to drink in large volumes, hypotonic drinks are ideal for hot weather rides, but it's important to also replace carbohydrate in these conditions (e.g. water, very weak squash, lo-cal/diet/lite brands)

- Hypertonic: Slowest of all the fluids to empty from the gut to the bloodstream. Typically with a carbohydrate content of more than 10 per cent, due to their slow release nature, hypertonic fluids can actually hinder hydration. These drinks are best saved for post-ride refuelling with carbohydrate and protein (e.g. protein recovery powders, high-concentrate carbo drinks)

Drinking on the bike

For rides of about one hour plain water is perfectly adequate and if you can do without squash, your bottles will last a lot longer and be less prone to staining and mould deposits. Over one hour and it is worth diluting water with a carbohydrate-based energy powder. In hot conditions it can also be worth adding electrolytes of sodium and potassium to replace the salts lost through sweating. After the ride it's more important to rehydrate with water or squash than electrolytes.

Gear your liquid intake to the weather. On hot days your two bottles might be one of a carb/electrolyte mix and the other pure water. The water is good to drink and ensures that your stomach stays in isotonic balance with your body fluids, but, when it's very hot, pure water is also of benefit to pour over yourself and cool your body.

Body temperature has important performance consequences. Your blood transports oxygen and fuel to your muscles, but your body also uses blood to dissipate heat by diverting it to the skin, where heat loss occurs through radiation. More blood going to the skin means less blood going to your working muscles, so they get less oxygen and fuel. The net result is that your power drops.

If you can keep cool another way, you preserve blood supplies to your muscles and they keep producing power. So, in something like the Etape du Tour, which is often run off in hot weather, wear light-textured and light-coloured clothing and use some of your water to pour over your head and legs.

TIP

If your race is in a hot country and you are training in the cold, travel there early to acclimatise, or do some sessions on a turbo at home with the heating on, so that your sweat reflex makes the adaptations you need, to maintain performance in hot weather.

DRINKING ON THE MOVE

· Cycling drinking bottles come in a range of sizes, generally between 500ml and one litre.

· With two bottle cages fitted you could carry two litres of fluid, enough for about four hours riding.

· For rides of up to two hours a single cage with a 750ml or one litre bottle would be sufficient.

· Two litres of water weighs two kilograms – the same weight as a lightweight frame and rear wheel!

· For off-road events a liquid-carrying bladder system, fitted to a custom-made back-sack is well worth considering. Drinking is done from a tube located near the mouth. You can carry three litres in a typical bladder system like a Camelbak. It's a better way to transport fluids on an endurance ride over rough terrain where bottles can be tricky to handle and can bounce out of a bottle cage.

Portion sizes

If you are trying to lose weight there is no better method than eating less, and the best way to eat less is to control portion size. One way to do that is eat off a smaller plate. Another tip is to eat slowly, because you have to eat for a while before your hunger reflex stops sending you messages.

Another golden rule for dieters is to divide your plate in two. One-half should be made up of salad, vegetables (not potatoes) and/or fruit. Split the other half into two again: one-half of that should be carbs (low glycaemic are best) and the other protein.

A useful diet tip is to start a meal with soup, as this helps fill you up without adding too many calories. Soups are great sources of vitamins and minerals too, because nothing is lost during their cooking. In fact up until quite recently and the introduction of protein shakes, minestrone soup was the staple post-training ride recovery food of professional cyclists.

Post-training protein and carbs

At the end of a ride your body is crying out for carbs, protein, vitamins and minerals to start the recovery and repair work needed to fully assimilate the work you've just done. The biggest need is carbohydrate, but research has proved that carbs are assimilated quicker by the body if they are eaten with some protein. A tuna or peanut butter sandwich is a very good post-ride snack as it contains carbs and protein, so your body can get on with refuelling and repair, and omega fatty acids that reduce inflammation and consequent muscle stiffness.

A good day's eating plan

TIP

In races only use food and drinks that you are used to. If a cyclo-sportive event provides free race food, find out what it is and train with it first.

TABLE 7.1: TRAINING DAY EATING PLAN

Breakfast	Porridge or muesli with milk or yoghurt, with a spoonful of whey protein added to it. Include some fruit with your cereal. Also, if you are having a heavy training day, eat one or two scrambled eggs on toast.
Snacks	Depends on training time, but if you are training in the morning you should take one or two energy bars or gels with you. Drink enough liquid to keep well hydrated, and if you finish training a long time before your lunch then consider a protein recovery drink or bar. Protein bars make good snacks at any time of day, but only eat one at a time – that means one in a morning and/or one in an afternoon.
Lunch	A homemade sandwich, soup or grilled meat or fish with pasta or rice. Try to eat some salad too, or drink some fruit juice.
Dinner	Much the same as lunch really, but this is another meal you should adjust to the amount of training you've done. It's also the time to try to boost your vitamin and mineral intake by eating a variety of salads or cooked vegetables. Fruit for dessert is good too. Anyone doing a block of hard training would also benefit from a pre-bedtime recovery drink. There are a number of these on the market and they are designed to drip-feed protein and other nutrients into your system as you sleep.

TABLE 7.2: RACE DAY EATING PLAN

Breakfast	Time this to be three hours before the race. The meal can be the same as on a training day for races from one to two hours, but for longer races consider adding pasta or rice with the scrambled eggs, and maybe topping that off with some Parmesan cheese. That is Lance Armstrong's favourite pre-race meal.
Travelling to the race	Sip a carbohydrate drink and eat an energy bar up to an hour before the start. Drink plain water too, especially on hot days. If you like it, a strong black coffee just before the race helps get you in the right frame of mind and it can help the release of fatty acids that your body uses as fuel. If you feel hungry before the race just take a bite of energy bar or eat a banana, but nothing more.
After the race	Rehydrate and eat. You might not feel like it, but it's a must. Recovery drinks are quite palatable nowadays, so research the market, pick one you like and get it down you as soon after the race finish as possible. Then when you feel a little more human again eat a protein recovery bar or a sandwich. Cheese is good as it is light on your stomach and easy to digest.
Dinner	Good quality protein and plenty of carbs, but don't go mad, and fresh salad or veg, just as you would on normal training days.

TIP

You need to eat more on cold days. The body will burn extra calories maintaining body temperature and glycogen stores will run low at a faster rate. A bigger pre-ride meal as well as an extra snack, energy drink or gel on the bike will ensure that you do not run low on energy earlier than on a temperate day.

TIP

Note for stage racers: Try to eat half a protein bar during the last hour of a stage, and make sure your recovery drink has protein in it. A pre-bedtime recovery drink is a great idea for stage racers.

Fuel on the bike, food and drink

Take care of your hydration needs with carbohydrate and electrolyte drinks. In cold or medium temperature conditions drink one big bottle for races between 30 and 50 miles; two bottles will do up to 75 miles. The advantage of carbohydrate in the drink is that you are refuelling at the same time as you drink. For races over 75 miles you will need more bottles handed up to you as the race progresses.

Your drinking strategy changes in hot weather. For between 30 and 50 miles take one bottle of carb drink and one of pure water. Above 50 miles and you are going to need more carb drinks and water handed up.

For a race below 30 miles just ensure you drink enough beforehand, but stop drinking 15 to 20 minutes before the start. This will give you the chance to relieve yourself of any excess. There is little point carrying a 750ml bottle for an event lasting about one hour, but a half-filled 500ml bottle with a carbo energy drink can provide a thirst quenching hit of energy halfway through the event.

TIP

Inside the last two miles of any race, if you are in a position to do well and have any liquid in your bottle, take a sip and pour the rest away so you are as light as possible for the finale of the race.

TIP

Practise eating and drinking on your bike in training so that it becomes second nature in a race.

As far as solid foods are concerned, what you eat depends on the length of your event. One thing, though: science has taken leaps and bounds in this direction and sports-specific energy bars and gels deliver exactly what you need in a form that is easy to digest, so we recommend going with them. For races up to 50 miles you'll be fine with a couple of gels. Over that and an energy bar, maybe two, and two or three gels are good up to 70 miles. Add a bar and a gel for each 25-mile chunk after 75 miles.

Plan your eating in long races by eating bars first then going on to gels later in the event. Watch your intake of gels though. Look for ones that are isotonic, or drink plain water after sucking one down. Gels are very concentrated and as you get dehydrated they can slow down the rate at which your stomach empties. So, you could be eating but not feel the benefit.

GELS

An energy gel packs a hit of energy and carbohydrate in a portable and digestible form. An energy gel is easily carried in a back pocket or tucked under a lycra short or sleeve. There are various brands, from PowerBar to High5 and SiS, some with caffeine for a boost of energy late in an event. Some are also isotonic and need not be taken with a mouthful of water, unlike many other gels which can leave a sticky residue if not washed down. Gels can be an effective way to maintain carbohydrate intake during an event, with between one and two required each hour.

Supplements

There is a lot of debate about supplements and they shouldn't really be considered until you have done all you can do to ensure you have a balanced diet of fresh food, with plenty of fresh fruit and veg. Remember, five-a-day is a minimum for an athlete. As we've already said, fish oils are a good supplement for any athlete, and if you aren't sure you are getting all you need then a multi-vitamin tablet with minerals will do you no harm, and it will increase your confidence.

If you feel you are lacking a particular nutrient then visit a doctor or dietician to discuss your suspicions. Women and older athletes have some specific supplement needs: again, these are best discussed with a dietician.

TIP

Take one more gel than you need on any race over 50 miles, to ensure that you can top-up your glycogen level if it starts to run low near the end of the event.

Eating sensibly

Nutrition is one thing that cyclists sometimes get seriously wrong. You will hear about extreme diets, wonder foods and super supplements, but for most cyclists good nutrition is a long haul made up of sticking to established sensible guidelines and following them day after day. Your focus should be on eating a variety of fresh foods from all the food groups, balancing your carbohydrate and protein intake with the work you do, and cutting saturated (bad) fats while boosting your intake of good fats like seeds and seed oil, olive oil, nuts and fish oils.

If you need to lose weight your best weapon is cutting portion size, and you should take the long view of weight loss. OK, you'll have heard of pro racers who do crazy things and lose weight in a very short time, but they sometimes have to do that and have a support network of qualified people to help them. If you don't have to, then don't. Just keep an eye on your weight by weighing yourself once a day at the same time and in the same clothes (none is best), and slightly adjust what you eat in the next 24 hours according to what the scales say. Then do the same again tomorrow, and the day after that and the day after that.

Think of food as the stuff that keeps you on the road, and keeping on the road means doing more training. If you do more training you will improve. Think about it – you can't train and improve if you are always ill or injured. So in the long term, keeping going is the one thing we all have the ability to do that will help us improve. Keeping going and the long haul should be the watchword of your nutritional strategy: eat for today, tomorrow and the following weeks and months, by eating consistently and sensibly.

RIDER STORY

Dan Martin is a professional with the Garmin Transitions team.

'I would never have thought of being checked out for food intolerances or allergies. My dad was a pro racer and my uncle won the Tour de France (Dan's uncle is Stephen Roche, Tour winner in 1987), so I was brought up in a house that understood what a bike racer needs to eat and appreciated the value of good healthy food and a balanced diet. And because of that I never had to think about my diet. I bet I've not had a McDonalds more than five times in my life.

'But in my second year as a pro I developed a digestive problem that wouldn't clear up. The team suggested I have a tolerance test and those tests found I was wheat intolerant. I went wheat-free and it was like some-body had flipped a switch. Immediately I felt a lot more comfortable after eating, and I didn't seem to have any ups and downs in energy any more.

'When I was an amateur in France all we ate was pasta. I always felt bloated after a meal, but I thought it was normal because I was eating a lot of food to replace the energy I'd burned up. Now I stick to rice and potatoes, and occasionally butternut squash and quinoa for my carbs.

'Then I got thinking about other aspects of my diet and I've cut down on sugary stuff, even in races. We did some tests and found that I can ride at quite a high level of effort and still burn fats instead of sugar.

'So tests can be worth having if you have a specific digestive problem. I'm still not like a monk with my eating though. Where I live in Girona there is a great Irish bar that does good burgers. If I haven't got a race coming up I go and have a burger and the bread and chips, and a beer. I feel that I've had bread next day, but you can't have a burger without bread, can you?'

From endurance to power

How do you go from four months of endurance training into your first big challenge of the season without getting blown away on the first hill? The answer is that you mix your endurance rides with increasing amounts of top-end sessions which simulate the intensity of effort required to rip up a climb or sprint out of a corner. When the action kicks off you want to be tuned up physically and mentally for the challenge.

In Chapter 4 we covered the foundation work laid during the four-month block between the end of the summer season and the following spring, when the calendar cranks back into action. The new season starts the day after your final event of the previous one. Even if you take a holiday or a complete break from all exercise, your mental hard drive will appreciate the reboot and once training resumes, enthusiasm levels should be sky-high.

But winter can drag and while you may have every intention of following an endurance-based training programme, incorporating interval sessions after the first two months of base training, it helps to have alternative strategies. One way to ensure that you maintain high levels of top-end throughout the winter is to race cyclo-cross, mountain bike cross-country or indoor track. There is even a growing trend towards winter road racing on closed circuits. A one-hour race every week is a great way to break up the endurance rides, with threshold efforts and more demanded by a race scenario.

Many cyclists use turbo trainers, spinning classes and rollers to stay fit indoors when the conditions make riding outside pointless or too hazardous. There are endless turbo sessions out there – we will give examples of the most effective workouts which can be used to home in on some very specific areas of intensity.

With spring around the corner the desire to get outside and put all the hard work to the test is a feeling familiar to every competitive cyclist. A training camp in warm weather can be a great way to put the finishing touches to your training and if you approach it right, could set you up for the rest of the season. Get it wrong and illness and the symptoms of overtraining can hobble all the graft put in over the previous four months.

Think about rest as part of your
training – if you work hard and
rest hard you will improve.

Race off-road

Cyclo-cross has got it all as a training aid: it mixes the highest levels of intensity aerobically and anaerobically; it's an endurance workout that lasts around one hour; it's great for bike handling skills and confidence; and it's a lot of fun. That's the good news. The bad news is that it can be horribly wet, cold and muddy, it takes one day out of your weekend when you could be putting in a much longer base endurance ride, and it can lead to overtraining if you are also putting in the hours during the week. Oh, and you need to have at least one cyclo-cross-specific bike, or a mountain bike, to do it on.

But as a way to get you through the winter and out the other side with excellent top-end and aerobic fitness, cross is hard to beat. It's also a very friendly and inclusive sport, with mixed fields of 100 or more riders of every ability setting off together, with each rider given a final position no matter how far behind they finish. A cyclo-cross event takes place on an off-road short circuit, often based around a playing field or park, with a mix of terrain including short sharp climbs, sand pits and technical wooded sections. Quite often there is at least one obstacle that requires the riders to dismount and run over or up.

Sounds hard? Yes it is: for every rider in a cyclo-cross the effort required to hold your place is as close to the anaerobic threshold as you can get. Each little acceleration, up a climb, exiting a corner or running over barriers, pushes the system into anaerobic territory. These short efforts may last for less than 10 seconds and rarely exceed 30, but they surpass anything you will attain during a winter interval session. As if that were not enough of a workout, cross also exercises your upper body whenever you dismount, shoulder the bike, and run with it. The current trend is for courses which favour riding with only a minimum of running, but that does not stop you from working your core and arms by running with your cross bike in training.

Bike handling skills will also be tested to the full on your cross bike. During the course of a season you will encounter every type of surface and terrain, in wet and dry conditions, and even during a race there will be changes in the character of the course as well as chances for you to practise different lines and techniques.

Cross races are sociable affairs: they normally take place around the middle of the day on Sundays and the short circuit layout makes them spectator-friendly. There are usually events for youth categories, followed by the main race for male and female seniors, juniors and veterans. For families of cyclists, cross is perfect as everyone can get a race in the space of three hours or so.

Cyclo-cross bike tips

- Tubular tyres are by far the best choice for grip and puncture resistance. They can be run at very low pressures, right down to the low 20s on the front tyre. As a general rule, run the lowest pressures you can on any given course. Make sure tubulars are very well glued on and use a separate tyre pressure gauge for the most accurate reading. For conditions ranging from sand to mud to dry trails, it's worthwhile having at least two sets of wheels with tread patterns suitable for high- and low-grip scenarios. Fat tyres are best for cross but 35c wide is the maximum permitted.

- Clincher tyres (high pressure beaded tyres) cannot be run at pressures as low as tubulars and around 35psi is about the softest you would ever want to risk on the front. Unlike tubulars, which are not prone to pinch flats, clinchers are easily punctured if the rim hits a tree root or similar raised edge. It is possible to fit a puncture-resistant band to a clincher and even use a liquid sealant, both of which would allow pressures to be run a few psi lower.

- Saddle height can be lowered by 1cm compared to your road bike position. This lowers your centre of gravity and makes remounting easier. A more upright position with a stem 1cm shorter than your road setup will also help to control the bike in technical sections.

- Slightly wider bars than your road bars make it easier to perform the bigger direction changes demanded by cross racing. The brake levers can also be positioned higher up the bars for greater comfort and control. Unlike a road bike there is no advantage in adopting an aerodynamic posture, as you will not be travelling fast enough off-road.

- A cassette with a range of gears – you need some big sprockets as low as 28 on the back – is relatively easy to find, but chainsets with the correct rings are not so common. Compact chainsets are not ideal as the 50 ring is too big and 34-tooth inner ring is too small. A popular chainring choice for cyclo-cross is 36–46.

- Do not use an ultra-lightweight saddle as you need something with fairly strong rails and a padded top which can take your full weight when you jump back onto the bike, ideally in one airborne acrobatic movement.

- Change chains before they start to wear the chainrings and rear cassette: you will get a lot more life out of the rings and sprockets. It's also worth changing the cables at the beginning of each season, although fitting sealed ones is worth the extra expense.

- If you do not have a cyclo-cross bike then in local events you can normally ride a mountain bike. A light mountain bike can be hustled around a cyclo-cross course quickly enough but they are not easy to lift and carry on the shoulder, and despite appearances they can be harder work than a cross bike over soft ground due to their energy-sapping fat tyres.

How cross can fit into your winter endurance programme

A typical week for a rider who is training for the summer but wants to include cyclo-cross in their preparation is shown in table 8.1.

TABLE 8.1: WEEKLY TRAINING PROGRAMME	
Monday	Easy day
Tuesday	One minute max effort
Wednesday	A hilly road ride
Thursday	A longer, steadier ride
Friday	Easy day
Saturday	Cyclo-cross race
Sunday	Long road ride, intervals, either on road or turbo

If your cyclo-cross race is on a Sunday it isn't so convenient, because you need to get the long rides in during the winter. You could do one on Saturday, but that will leave you tired for Sunday's race. One solution would be an easy day Thursday and a long ride Friday.

Training for the cyclo-cross specialist

The peak of the cyclo-cross season is January to early February, when the national and world championships are held. So downtime for cross riders comes in February or March, depending on their objectives, when a rest from rigorous training should be scheduled.

Begin training again in April with a period of steady riding, decreasing the distance and upping the tempo as the month progresses. Serious cyclo-cross riders should race on the road as it improves their speed. Start a couple of weeks into April and continue through to the start of the cross season in September; from July try to ride in as many criteriums as possible because the effort required for them is similar to what's needed in a cyclo-cross race.

Cyclo-cross training starts in mid-August. Begin by introducing some running into your training, doing short distances at first but building to 30 minutes three times a week until September. Then cut your running to two sessions a week: either 20 minutes fast or 30 minutes of intervals. Include uphill and downhill running in your training.

Start doing a few long rides, some of them on a mountain or cyclo-cross bike, and go off-road to practise some of the skills you need for cyclo-cross, like dismounting and running with the bike. These long rides will help you build a bank of stamina and resistance that you can draw on during harder, shorter and more specific training.

Late summer kick-off

Specific cross training starts in mid August. Do two sessions a week of short intervals or threshold efforts, either on the road or on a turbo, or try an off-road session like Roger Hammond's. Lean towards longer, anaerobic threshold intervals at the start of specific training, then do shorter above-threshold ones as training progresses to mid November.

That is when you should top up your stamina again with some longer rides, maybe even not racing for a couple of weekends to fit two long rides in. Many top cyclo-cross pros go on a warm weather training camp at this point during their race season. What you are doing is recharging the stamina bank ready for the push to the highpoint of the season and the various championships.

Specific cyclo-cross sessions start again at the beginning of December. Again, do threshold efforts first and build the intensity over three weeks while cutting back the distance of each interval. A turbo session of 30 seconds flat out with one-minute recovery, repeated 10 to 20 times, is a great session to help build to a peak now. Then you can use the Christmas period, when there are a number of races on the holiday days, to arrive at top form by racing two, three or even four times in a seven-day period. If you do this, though, cut out all other interval training and just ride steady in between races.

Now you are ready for the national championships. If you have objectives after those, continue doing the specific cross efforts off-road and short, hard intervals between your races to maintain form.

I have mapped out a short circuit on grass. There's a run up a bank, some flat bits, a few dead turns, another short hill I climb on the bike and a couple of descents. It takes about three minutes to ride flat out.

What I do is ride out to the circuit for a warm-up. Then I do three sets of ten minutes going as hard as I would in a race on the circuit, with five minutes easy between sets. Then I ride home to cool down.

Roger Hammond, multinational cyclo-cross champion and pro road racer

Mountain biking

At one time it looked like mountain bike cross-country racing was going to become the dominant form of knobbly tyres competition. It never happened: despite a healthy professional scene through the 1990s, the last 10 years have seen the cross-country discipline overtaken by downhill and non-competitive freeriding.

Cross-country racing is mostly a summer sport, with longer marathon events becoming increasingly popular. There are some winter events and series, often based around closed-road circuits, which can be used for a workout similar to a cyclo-cross event. The physical and technical challenges are roughly the same, with short intense bursts of power mixed with low-stress sections where all you are trying to do is stay on board.

But just because you cannot race your mountain bike, that should not deter you from making use of it throughout the winter. As a way to continue cycling when you are getting bored with the road, or when conditions on the road are too hazardous for cyclists (snow and ice), a ride into the woods or across the fields on a mountain bike is a great way to continue training.

Park and ride

If you have access to some land where you can mark out or imagine a short circuit, then a mountain bike can be used for interval training or hill sprints. If it's a park with lighting why not schedule a 45-minute interval session once a week after work? As Lance Armstrong has shown with his successful, though occasional, forays into marathon mountain bike events, riding off-road is also one of the best ways to hone pedalling technique.

Mountain bikers have been shown to have one of the most even power strokes of any cyclist, with an extremely smooth transition between the power-on and power-off segments of the pedal stroke. A smooth and jerk-free pedalling action is less likely to break traction off-road and it won't do your road riding any harm at all. Pedalling at higher cadences – the only way to make progress in sticky or technical going off-road – is also a skill that benefits from polishing and perfecting in the off season.

Mountain biking can be hard on the body and the risk of injury from crashing is also ever-present. If you are not a dedicated mountain bike racer it's important to ride conservatively off-road, keeping the risks to a minimum. It may feel safe when you are far from road traffic and riding on soft ground, but hidden rocks, low branches and tree stumps can turn an innocent tumble into something much more serious.

Riding alone in isolated areas adds to the risk of injury or damage to the bike – always carry a mobile phone with you and wear a helmet. Carry water and energy food and a waterproof top.

Winter track racing and fixed wheel riding

If you live near a banked cycling track or velodrome, not only are you very lucky, but you also have a facility that is virtually guaranteed to improve your cycling. Track riding is acknowledged as the purest cycling discipline, with sprint and endurance events that demand the highest levels of cycling fitness and technique. All but the most specialised match sprinters can take skills they have learned on the track and make them work successfully for them on the road.

Even if you just train on an outdoor track on dry days through the winter, you can schedule your intervals and fitness tests for those days and ensure that you are replicating the same conditions virtually every time. This guarantees a pretty accurate record of your ongoing condition as you fill in your training diary.

More fun is to ride on an indoor velodrome, racing in a winter track league in a variety of events which give you an endurance, speed and sprint workout. If you are weak at sprinting, the track is a good place to work on your leg speed, racing tuck and track skills. You do not have to ride in match sprint events against the specialists: a points or scratch race will pit you against a bunch of endurance riders, just like in a road race.

Above all, the opportunity to ride on the track in winter, even if it's just a few times in the run-up to Christmas for instance, will be tremendous fun and a great learning process. Chances are that you will not be competing regularly on the track in the four-month winter period; if you are then your summer season would need to reflect that. The same goes for serious cyclo-cross riders – there are not many cyclists who can sustain a 12-month nonstop year of racing without, at some point, planning for periods of complete rest and recovery.

Singlespeed

One of the benefits of track riding is the opportunity to ride a fixed gear – a single fixed sprocket on the rear wheel which dictates that the rider pedals all the time the rear wheel is turning. Fixed gear bikes are the simplest of machines and a track bike is the most basic of all, with the minimum of components: no brakes, no derailleur gears and nothing on the bars to operate either system. A road based fixed gear bike just needs to have brakes added, and maybe a set of mudguards for winter riding. Both machines can be put together relatively cheaply compared to a geared bike and there are numerous affordable 'fixie' bikes on the market today. As a way to perfect your pedalling technique, nothing beats a fixed wheel.

Fixed wheel road bikes are well suited to commuting as they are low-maintenance machines which fare much better than geared bikes in grotty winter conditions. Get the gear right and you can spin along at 100rpm in the high teens mph, staying warm and achieving the ultimate pedalling masterclass.

FACT

Raw speed and acceleration are the most important factors in almost every branch of bike racing.

Turbo training

For many cyclists, especially those in northern climes, the modern turbo trainer has become an indispensable aid to training. Fluid trainers are quiet and affordable with higher spec models fitted with power meters, speed, distance and cadence counters, heart rate monitors, and flat screens displaying information and moving images. A regular turbo session can be an effective way to supplement your on-road endurance programme. In terms of monitoring your effort it's a very controllable way to work through a progression of interval sessions, at anaerobic threshold and beyond, without going over the top.

For time-hungry cyclists the turbo can be the only way to maintain contact with the bike during a busy winter period, when there may only be enough time for some cross training and a few 30-minute sessions on the turbo. Maintain general fitness levels through this time with cross training and stay in touch with the pedals on the turbo – if there's no choice this will get you through a busy period.

Keep it interesting

Sounds too good to be true? There is a downside to turbo training: it can get very boring. If you have decided upon using a turbo as a regular part of your training it's well worth setting it up somewhere you can listen to music or, even better, watch a race DVD or film. Anything that gives your brain something to keep it stimulated during a session is worth considering – even if it means reading a book on a stand in front of the bars!

Make sure the room is well ventilated or that you have a fan near to hand which can be turned up or down, depending on the level of effort. The body generates lots of heat on the turbo: the sweat starts to pour off and a fan helps to keep you cool and dry. Drink plenty of fluid and drape a towel over the bars and top tube to stop the sweat corroding the paint. Turbo training can be hard on the bike, especially if the front wheel is also fixed to the device. If you can use an old bike with a turbo-specific rear tyre, that machine can stay in the turbo and thus save your best bike from stresses that don't occur in normal road riding.

How long you ride the turbo for each session depends on your early season goals and your tolerance of indoor riding. On average a session will last from 30 minutes to one hour and, depending on the nature of the session, even 30 minutes of hard intervals could leave you completely spent. Super-motivated cyclists can endure two hours or more, but you have to be very determined to stick to a worthwhile session without drifting down to low-level endurance training. Best to keep an indoor session short, structured and satisfyingly hard.

Rollers

An alternative to the turbo trainer is rollers, which have come back into fashion in recent times, having been previously only viewed as a warm-up device for track riders. Rollers cost similar money to turbo trainers but instead of riding the bike on a rear-wheel-mounted resistance device, the bike simply sits on three drums attached to a metal frame. Two drums sit under the back wheel and one under the front. There is nothing holding the bike up – that is all down to you.

Once the rider has mounted the bike by holding on to something solidly fixed with one hand and the bars with the other, the pedals are turned and, after some initial heart stopping lurches to the outer edges of the drum, it's surprisingly easy to pedal upright with the roller thrumming beneath the bike. The first few times you may well

drop off the edge of the rollers and for that reason it is worth having a hand-hold on both sides. Fear not, the bike will not shoot forwards and all you have to do to regain lost balance is put a hand on something stable like a table or wall.

Rollers are excellent for developing leg speed, which improves the energy efficiency in the muscles so that they rely less on glycogen, thus growing mitochondria and using oxygen more efficiently. The act of balancing on the rollers also gives the core muscles a good workout, because it is the muscles of your core that maintain your balance. Fast pedalling and improved core strength can complement turbo sessions aimed at power increases for a formidable indoor workout, but you might need to extend the shed first!

Rollers cannot provide the resistance that a turbo offers so in that sense they are not a true alternative in terms of developing power, although there is a brand of rollers available now with the same fan wind-resistance units as in some turbo trainers.

Turbo sessions

30-second to 60-second intervals

These are great for building sustained power and are probably best performed on a turbo.

- Warm up for 10 minutes then go as hard as you can for either 30 seconds or 60 seconds, just lasting the distance before you want to fall off your bike.
- Ride easy for twice the length of the interval and repeat.
- Start with 8–10 sets of 30 seconds and 4–5 of 60 seconds, working to a maximum of 20 for the shorter and 10 for the longer interval.
- This session is key in a lot of top riders' programmes.

The core session

- Warm up for 10 minutes then go flat out for 10 seconds, recover for 20 seconds and repeat for 15 minutes.
- This session improves your acceleration and your core strength; it is also excellent for conditioning you to a new race position.
- It is particularly important to use a time trial bike if you have been doing a lot of road racing and want to build some specific strength on this bike.

Threshold intervals

- Same warm-up as above then ride at your anaerobic threshold, determined by heart rate power or feel for 5 minutes.
- Go easy for 5 minutes and repeat this cycle three more times before doing 10 minutes easy to cool down.

FOCUS ON

Your objectives

When building for the season focus on the racing you want to do and the events you want to peak at. Don't follow other people's training but create your own programme, built from the relevant blocks of training logic that will ensure you arrive at your chosen events in top form. And hold on to that focus throughout your build-up.

Everyone, even a Tour de France champion like Alberto Contador, has days when they do not feel like doing a session. When that happens focus on what you want to achieve and what it will feel like afterwards: if that doesn't get you to start the session and see it through then you are probably tired and it's best to cut it short.

Duty of care

You need to look after yourself when in training. Don't train with a cold, illness or injury, or when you are really tired already and even thinking about your ambitions leaves you uninspired. But beware of letting excuses get in the way.

The great Irish champion Sean Kelly once said: 'You can't tell what the weather is like from inside the house. Go out and ride, then you'll know, but while you're out you may as well get your training done.' Kelly was an acknowledged hard case, and a great rider with the constitution of a horse, but his attitude never fails to impress.

See your plan through, don't chop and change. There are nuances to training for bike racing, but broadly speaking any progressive training programme containing sessions that increase your stamina, strength and riding speed over a variety of distances, as long as it also allows time to recover and is supported by good nutrition, will make you improve as a bike rider. Just focus on it, even in the hard times, or – better – especially in the hard times, and you'll be surprised at what you can achieve.

RIDER STORY

Dean Downing is a GB-based professional with Team Rapha-Condor.

'When I want to get my racing legs on again I do a version of a training session called Russian Steps on my rollers. You warm up then start with 15 seconds flat out and go easy for 15 seconds, then do 30 seconds flat out and easy for 30 and keep building that through one minute, two, three ... until five minutes flat out.

'Then you come down again, four flat out, four easy, three, two, one minute, 30 seconds and 15 seconds.'

'If I've been doing some road training in the winter and I have to ride a track race I'll do Russian Steps a couple of times during the week before.

'Another thing though is that I do a lot of my training with a group. We'll ride steady maybe for an hour then pick it up until halfway. Go easy again and pick it up again half an hour before the finish.

'Thing is though, one group I ride with on a Tuesday has enough good riders in it for a top road race. So part of my Tuesday session, and the Saturday one sometimes, is always like racing.'

Peaking for summer

From spring onwards the main cycling season, on the road and for mountain biking and amateur track, fills the diary with endless opportunities to test yourself and race others. It's quite possible to race or ride a challenge event three times a week during the summer if you are really keen. A big race or sportive on Sunday can be followed by a track league event on Tuesday and a club time trial on Thursday. That would be a heavy schedule, especially for a rider holding down a job and with family commitments.

While enthusiasm can be sky-high it pays to remember that even professional riders would not be able to sustain a multiple-race week without plenty of rest and a back-up team behind the scenes monitoring health, massaging legs, washing kit and fettling bicycles. Regular riders need to bear this in mind and do everything possible to organise, rest and plan breaks for recovery and for top-up training.

Ride at full throttle three times a week every week and you will soon start to feel the strain. Even top riders with back-up have goals plotted through the season, giving them opportunities to plan phases of their training and racing which allow for alternating periods of intensity. Periodisation may have fallen out of favour in some quarters but it still has relevance when the intention is to maintain a high performance level over several months.

It's important to start with targets, big ones and secondary ones, which form the peaks of a season. Then there are periods of tapering, build-up and rest, and time off, which could be a holiday or just time off the bike. It's also important during a busy season to remind yourself why you love cycling and that, whatever your results and some inevitable disappointments, there is no shame in taking a break or changing your season plan. Quite often the ability to recognise the signs of low morale and staleness can result in a much better return to form.

Periodisation

Periodisation is an approach to training that many coaches swear by and, although there are reservations about how widely to apply it to a training schedule, there is no doubt that the basics make a lot of sense. As it says on the tin, periodisation is about planning periods of specific training and rest in a variety of short- to long-term programmes. There are three time frames into which a periodisation coaching plan can fit: macrocycles, mesocycles and microcycles.

The central idea of periodisation is to build up for a specific race as you would build a pyramid, with a big base made up of endurance training. On top of that you place a narrower layer of harder training, and follow that with a peak of really fast stuff to bring you to top form. Each layer underpins and prepares you for the next, and doing them in the order of endurance to speed is thought to be the correct way for your body to make the adaptations it needs for a top performance.

Most cyclists will build two or three pyramids of form throughout the year. If their racing season is during the summer they will build the biggest pyramid during the winter to prepare for spring racing, but then add a couple more, going back to doing some more endurance work, adding harder stuff to it and popping another peak of speed work on top of that.

Macrocycles

This often refers to a full cycling season or year and it can even be imposed on a four or five year build-up to something like an Olympics or a once-in-a-lifetime goal. Basically, though, each periodised pyramid you build is a macrocycle, so you might have one to cover a single objective for the year, or more if you have several objectives. For example, a good standard road racer might build one pyramid to peak for the local area championship, then begin another for the nationals, and after that perhaps consider another for an end of season objective.

Mesocycles

From two to six weeks, this type of periodisation makes up the building blocks of training and competition. For a serious cyclist these blocks are:

- Foundation, or preparation
- Pre-competition, or transition
- Competition and recovery

Microcycles

These divide the mesocycle into bite-size units of from one week to a fortnight. Each cycle has a specific goal, which can be to perfect a riding skill or specific area of fitness. It can also relate to a tapering period in the run-up to a big target event and will be structured to deliver the rider in a rested state, yet fresh and in top form.

Year planner

The year planner in table 9.1 gives examples of how you could divide your year if you were aiming to peak for a major race, sportive or other challenge event in early July. There is also a build-up to an event, like a stage race or multi-day sportive, at the end of May, followed by a short recovery period, then a second build-up in the run-up to a major goal at the end of the second macrocycle.

TABLE 9.1: YEAR PLANNER

MESOCYCLE	RECOVERY MESOCYCLE	PREPARATION MESO-CYCLE #1	PREPARATION MESO-CYCLE #2	PREPARATION MESO-CYCLE #3	TRANSITION MESO-CYCLE PRIOR TO RACING	RACING MESO-CYCLE #1	RACING MESO-CYCLE #2	RACING MESO-CYCLE #3
ACTIVITY	Easy rides	Progressive build-up of long, steady distance rides. Progressive work on strength and areas of weakness			Speed training (anaerobic)	Racing. Progressively longer distances and greater intensity, interspersed with short-distance speed work and rest		
						MINOR PEAK ▼	**MAJOR EVENT** ▼	
TRAINING ZONE	Zones 1–2	Mainly Zones 1–2, occasionally Zone 3			Mostly training Zones 3–4	Racing in Zones 4–5 Training in Zones 3–5 Tapering to peak for specific goals towards the end of each meso-cycle with recovery week after each peak		
TRAINING PHASE	Recovery	Preparation			Pre-comp	Competition		
MONTH	OCT	NOV	DEC	JAN	FEB	MAR	APR	MAY	JUN	JUL	AUG	SEP

By dividing the periods into less daunting macrocycles, you can aim to bring yourself to peak condition at the end of each period. Between consecutive periods is a good time to take a short rest and recuperate from the efforts leading up to the target event at the end of the previous cycle.

Microcycles are not covered in this plan because their shortness creates a heap of detail and the whole point of a microcycle is that it allows the rider to adjust training in the short term and according to individual circumstances. Note that the plan does not run from January to December but follows a more realistic cyclist's year from October to September.

Table 9.2 shows a typical summer training plan: it assumes a big mesocycle to build up endurance carried out during the winter, by following the schedules we included in Chapter 5. This plan would work for a road racer, especially if they added a little distance to keep up endurance levels, or for a short-distance time triallist. The days you do the work are suggestions and you should rearrange them to fit your own circumstances. From week five onwards a mid-week race can be substituted for one of the interval or threshold training sessions. March would be a good time to start this plan.

TIP

Training in a paceline group, like a chain gang in breakaway or team time trial-style, is great for adding speed to your training.

FOCUS ON

Being adaptable

Planning your training is like planning a journey. You won't get where you want to be unless you take time to prepare a route beforehand. We're talking pre-GPS days now! You must plan, and plan meticulously, but your plan should be adapted to your situation, and don't let your ambitions be totally derailed if things go wrong.

The training plans we've given you are based on a classic 'train three days mid-week and train/race at weekends' pattern. It's a good one that gives you two rest days to space out the week's work and to let your body assimilate the training you've done. It's ideal for people working nine to five, five days a week, with the weekend off. But not everyone does that.

So, if you work shifts, or you travel and can't take your bike with you, you need to take the elements of a training plan and fit them into your week, or better still a two-week period. You'll still end up doing the same amount of work. And don't forget the rest days: they are as important as training. In fact they are training and have to be done just as conscientiously as the toughest interval session.

Every now and again a spanner gets thrown in the works and you will miss one or two sessions, or maybe a whole week. If that happens, forget it. Don't try and do extra in the next session or week, just carry on as though it hadn't happened and put it down to having some extra rest.

While we are on the subject of resting, it's worth saying again that good, fresh food in a balanced diet is just as important as rest and training. One thing, though: there is a lot of talk about recovery drinks, but these are dense in calories. Use them by all means but keep an eye on your weight and cut back at meal times if you see weight going on.

HOW THE PROS DO IT

Most professional cyclists nowadays have coaches, or some kind of trainer, who can sit down and plan with. The actual training they do and their training year will depend on what sort of rider they are.

Team leaders for the Classics train very differently from those who will lead the teams in the Grand Tours. Classics riders look at maximising their VO_2max, increasing their maximum power and lactate tolerance, and sharpening up their sprint. Tour riders work on stretching their endurance, increasing the intensity they can work at using fats as fuel, increasing their speed at anaerobic threshold, and being as skinny as they can be.

But when you look at even the top end of world cycling there are very few riders on programmes as specialised as this, because there are only a handful that can win Grand Tours and maybe a couple of handfuls in the Classics. As for the rest, they are helpers, either for the Classics or for the sprinters in stage races, or a few are super domestiques who help Grand Tour racers in the mountains. Some of them have very specialised plans with clearly defined objectives, but most have to be all-rounders who need to be close to their best condition for a longer time each year, with the possibility of leading the team in lesser races from time to time as well.

These riders work with coaches too, but their programmes can change at the drop of a hat, and once at race fitness they add to, or take elements from, their training according to where their fitness is at that point in time and when they are next expected by the team to be going well.

Below professional-level racing there is another string of talented racers who sometimes have to race with pro riders, but for the rest of the time take part in lesser events. Their problem is they don't get the depth of racing that pro riders do, so they often simulate stage races by training twice a day for several days, or training through their races. What that means is they will begin a block of hard training on a Tuesday and train hard right up to the next weekend, when they might do two races. After that they train hard again on Monday and maybe for three further days, before backing off for Sunday's race. It's called overload, and it's another way of simulating a stage race.

But beware of copying the pros: their life is a balancing act between doing the training they need, to maximise their potential, and doing so much that they get ill or injured. Remember too that they have a team of backroom girls and boys whose only job is to keep them healthy. And be very wary of copying what the top pros do regarding eating. In fact don't do it. The big thing in pro bike racing, especially with Grand Tour contenders, is to be as skinny as possible. To be like that, each year the best riders will go through a period where their mantra is 'eating is cheating'. We've seen pros on a weight loss plan who are clammy-skinned and shaking from hunger.

Remember, though, that is all the pros have to do: their bodies are their tools and they understand how they work. These racers are also extremely robust, highly trained, and they have that team of qualified experts helping them. And they only do this for a limited period – even their Grand Tour weight is something that they can only keep up for the length of the race. It's not unusual for them to weigh six kilograms more two weeks after a big stage race finishes.

TIP

Training with riders who are better than you can make you improve, but it can damage your confidence too.

TABLE 9.2: TYPICAL SUMMER TRAINING PLAN

Week	Monday	Tuesday	Wednesday
1	Recovery ride (you can also do things like yoga and stretching on recovery days, and remember to keep up your core training all year)	Warm up for 15 min, then do 2 x 15–20 min @ solid level 3. Warm down for 15 min (always end training sessions with 10 to 15 min of easy riding)	Ride for 90 min @ level 2, with some level 3
2	Recovery ride	Warm up for 15 min, then do 3 x 5 min @ level 3–4. On flat or undulating road for time triallists and on a short circuit for road racers, who should attack the corners hard	Ride for 90 min @ level 2, with some level 3
3	Recovery ride	Warm up for 15 min. Road riders need a circuit of about 1 mile with four 90-degree bends. Do 3 x 10 min as if you were racing, sprinting out of each corner, 5 min easy between sets. Time triallists ride 2 x 4 miles as hard as you can, recording the times	Ride for 2 hours @ level 2, with some level 3
4	Recovery ride	Ride @ level 2–3 for 1 hour	Warm up for 15 min and do 10 x 1 min seated in the saddle, pushing quite a high gear, real power-building intervals (try to keep your upper body still during the intervals)
5	Recovery ride	Warm up for 15 min, then do 2 x 20 min @ solid level 3, pushing almost to level 4. Warm down for 15 min	Ride for 90 min @ level 2, with some level 3
6	Recovery ride	Warm up for 15 min. Road racers do 4 x 3 min as hard as you can go for 3 min, with 3 min between efforts. Time triallists ride 1 mile @ TT race pace, then 1 mile @ level 2, repeating that 5 times if 10 miles is your target event, 10 times if 25 miles	Ride for 90 min @ level 2, with some level 3. If you have more time and recovered well from yesterday then do more of this today

Thursday	Friday	Saturday	Sunday
Warm up for 15 min then do 3 x 3 min @ level 4, uphill if you are a road racer	Recovery ride	Ride for 1 hour @ level 2. Include 3 max sprints, with 5 min easy pedalling in a low gear between efforts	Race
Warm up for 15 min, then do 5 x 2 min uphill	Recovery ride	Ride for 1 hour @ level 2. Include 3 max sprints with 5 min easy pedalling in a low gear between sets. Then ride as hard as you can for 5 min	Race
Warm up for 15 min. Find a hill that is at least long enough to take 1 min riding as hard as you can and do 10 x 1 min up it	Recovery ride	Do 2 hours on undulating terrain @ level 2, 3 and 4 (not too much 4 though, just the tops of hills)	Repeat yesterday's session but try to ride further
Ride @ level 2–3 for 1 hour	Recovery ride	Ride for 1 hour @ level 2. Include 3 max sprints with 5 min easy pedalling in a low gear between efforts	Race. This is a test of your form so really give it some stick!
Warm up for 15 min. Road riders need a circuit of about 1 mile with four 90-degree bends. Do 3 x 10 min as if you were racing, sprinting out of each corner, 5 min easy between sets. Time trial-lists ride 2 x 4 miles as hard as you can, recording the times	Recovery ride	Race a 10 mile TT if possible. This is recommended for road racers and time triallists	Race
Warm up for 15 min, then do 2 x 20 min @ solid level 3, pushing almost to level 4. Warm down for 15 min	Recovery ride	Ride for 1 hour @ level 2. Include 3 max sprints with 5 min easy pedalling in a low gear between efforts. Then ride as hard as you can for 5 min	Race

TABLE 9.2: TYPICAL SUMMER TRAINING PLAN

Week	Monday	Tuesday	Wednesday
7	Recovery ride	Warm up for 15 min, then do 10 x 1 min power intervals (you can replace this with 15 x 30 sec intervals if increasing your power is a big objective). It doesn't hurt to do this one on a turbo – in fact it's better	Warm up for 15 min, then do 2 x 20 min @ solid level 3, pushing almost to level 4. Warm down for 15 min
8	Recovery ride	Ride for 90 min @ level 2, with some level 3	Recovery ride
9	Recovery ride	Race – summer track leagues, evening time trials and road races begin in Britain about the first week of May. Treat these as training sessions. Very valuable when you are trying to peak, but you'll have to alter your week, depending on what day races are in your area	Ride for 90 min @ level 2 with some level 3. If you have more time and recovered well from yesterday then do more of this today
10	Recovery ride	Race – good week for any rider to try a track league, or maybe a training session on the track, especially if it is motor-paced. Helps give you some extra zip as you approach your peak	Recovery ride
11	Recovery ride	Warm up for 15 min, then do 15 x 30 sec intervals in sets of 5 with 5 min easy between sets. Again, this is a good one for the turbo	Either race a time trial or simulate one
12	Recovery ride	Warm up for 15 min. Road racers do 2 x 3 min as hard as you can go for 3 min. Time triallists ride 3 miles flat out.	Ride @ level 2 for 1 hour

Thursday	Friday	Saturday	Sunday
Ride for 90 min @ level 2 with some level 3. If you have more time and recovered well from yesterday then do more of this today	Recovery ride	Race	Race
Ride for 90 min @ level 2, with some level 3. Do more if you have time and are feeling good	Recovery ride	Do 2 hours on undulating terrain @ level 2, 3 and 4 (not too much 4 though, just the tops of hills)	Repeat yesterday's session and do more if you are feeling good (this week gives your endurance a little boost before going into a peaking mesocycle)
Warm up for 15 min. Road racers do 3–5 x 3 min at the maximum you can hold for 3 min. Time triallists do 3–4 x 5 min at your anaerobic threshold	Recovery ride	Ride for 1 hour @ level 2. Include 3 max sprints with 5 min easy pedalling in a low gear between efforts. Then ride as hard as you can for 5 min	Race
Warm up for 15 min. Road racers do 4–5 x 3 min at the maximum you can hold for 3 min. Time triallists do 4 x 5 min at your anaerobic threshold	Recovery ride	Race	Race
Ride for 90 min @ level 2, with some level 3. If you have more time and recovered well from yesterday then do more of this today	Rest – no riding, do nothing	Have a fun ride. Just go for a coffee, maybe try a bit of mountain biking. Just enjoy yourself but try to fit in at least 2 hours of riding	Same as Saturday
Do your favourite hard training session. Keep the intensity of it but reduce the amount you ride at all intensities by 50%. You should end this session feeling pleasantly tired and good about your preparation for the big day	Rest – no riding, do nothing!	Ride for 1 hour easy. Include 3 max sprints with 5 min easy pedalling in a low gear between efforts. Then ride as hard as you can for 3 min	Rest, or ride @ level 4 for 40 min on a flat route

RIDER STORY

Julia Shaw is one of Britain's best open time trial racers, and also a masters world champion, despite working full time in a demanding job.

'Before I plan my training for the following year I look at what I achieved the previous year with my coach, not only in terms of my objectives for that year but where I finished relative to other riders in each race.

'We look at SRM power files for each race too. That way I can identify above and below par races for each time of the year and can look for reasons why they happened. We also do the same exercise halfway through the year, so we can adjust my training in the light of upcoming objectives.

'But I also have overall career goals I'd like to achieve, dream goals if you like, and I look at where I am in terms of them. That's pretty easy in time trialling as you have direct comparisons with your rivals. I do that because, although I have a masters world title, I still have ambitions in open, non-age group racing.

'Once I've looked at where I stand, I can think of ways to get faster. For example, I recently spent quite a bit of time, and money, being tested in a wind tunnel, and as a result of changes to my riding position I raced a lot faster.

'Then it's down to seeing where my target races are, so when I need to be at my best, counting back from them and planning my training. I'm experienced enough now to know what sort of training I should be doing in a build-up, and the order to do it in, so I put that training into my plan like building blocks, building to a peak for my big races.'

All out!

So you have followed a training plan, putting down a foundation of fitness in the winter followed by endurance, then adding power and speed training through the spring. You can't put it off any longer: the time has come to pull off the covers, emerge from the pits and give the motor a proper run-out against the opposition. That could mean your first race, or time trial or sportive. All require planning, commitment and preparation. It's natural that, as the big day nears, anticipation and excitement will turn to nervous energy.

Then there is the event itself. Cycle racing is much more interesting and nuanced than you might think when you are just watching it on the TV or by the roadside. Each type of cycling discipline has its own way of playing out, with various patterns of effort and tactics determining the result. At the simplest level a short time trial on road or track is a pure speed event, ridden at the highest pace that the rider can sustain over the set distance. Mass-start races and events on the road require guile and calculation, as well as physical prowess.

A sportive rider will almost certainly not be riding with the aim of finishing first, but there are still tactics and techniques to be employed if a good time and finishing position is the aim. The front groups of many sportives have become more and more like a road race 'peloton' – find yourself at the sharp end of one and you will be digging deep into your road race tactics bag.

Most people drive to events with their bike in or on top of the car and a kit bag crammed with clothing, race food and kit. Knowing what to pack and having a bag already half full can make the whole process of getting to an event much easier and quicker. Preparing a kit bag with emergency clothing and all-weather gear can really save the day.

Riding in a group

From training to sportives and road racing, the skills of group riding are the same, but can vary depending on road and weather conditions, and how co-operative each rider is feeling. Your first experience of riding in a group will most likely be when out training with as few as three other riders. In this scenario the foremost concerns are safety and co-operation.

Ride two abreast with the front two looking out for hazards and indicating them to the others, in plenty of time.

Keep a tight formation, riding elbow to elbow with no 'half-wheeling' – when one cyclist rides half a wheel ahead of the rider next to him.

Do not overlap the front wheel with the rear wheel of the rider in front. If he has to swerve, his back wheel will not go into yours.

Go through and off (see below), either in a 'stirring' pattern or by the front two riders pulling smartly off, then freewheeling to left and right while the second pair ride through the middle on to the front.

Do everything smoothly and predictably, especially when going through to the front. The idea is to maintain the constant pace of the group, not accelerate and slow down or do a much faster 'turn' on the front.

Going through and off with the front pair circulating down the outside of the group.

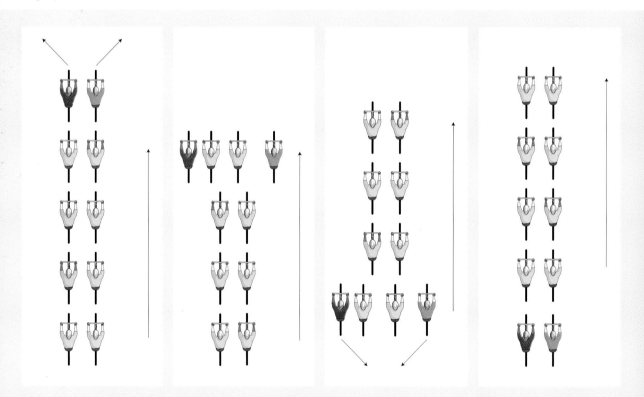

In a road race or sportive group situation there can be dozens of riders in a bunch, and quite often there will be riders in the group who either cannot or will not contribute to the pacemaking at the front. That does not mean that you cannot go through and off with those riders who are willing to maintain a constant high pace. Your work-shy rivals will merely gather behind the lines of pacemakers, taking advantage of your efforts. If it's any consolation the front of any bunch, the first 10 or so riders, is a much safer place to be than in the jostling group behind.

Wind direction can play a part when riding in a large hard-working road racing group. If the wind is blowing from one side, the line of riders in the wind will be the ones sliding back, while the sheltered side will contain the riders moving up the line to take their turn at the front. This form of echelon riding, which resembles two lines of geese in a flying formation, is only really possible on wide roads, where the group can form into two lines stretching from one side to the other.

TIP

If you aren't a good climber start every climb at or near the front, then if you slip back you will still be in the group and not behind it.

Pacemakers at the front of the bunch – it's hard work, but safer than in the pack itself.

Why ride hard at the front of a group?

Sitting behind another cyclist seriously reduces the amount of effort you have to make to keep up with the rider in front. It's been calculated that riders in big road race bunches can expend up to 40 per cent less energy thanks to the shelter provided by the other cyclists. That's an astounding figure, but it's understandable when you consider that wind resistance increases as the square of the bike's speed.

At low speeds, under 10mph, rolling resistance in the tyres and bearings is the main force slowing progress. But as the speed rises, wind or air resistance rapidly over-takes rolling resistance. Hit 25mph and 90 per cent of your effort is being spent just pushing you and your bike through the air. So why on earth would you wish to sit at the front of a group of cyclists taking advantage of your heroic efforts on the front?

- It's safer in front than in the centre of a bunch, where crashes are more frequent. On a twisty road or downhill the chance of a split means that you will be in the front group.

- If you want to escape the bunch you need to be at the front for long enough to choose the moment when, and the terrain on which, to launch an attack.

- You may be part of a team that is chasing a breakaway.

- On a hilly course the gains from drafting (sitting in the shelter of another rider) are reduced drastically when the speed drops on a climb and that is when it's vital to be as far forward as possible.

- Riding on the front is fun and a better workout than dodging turns further back. If everyone works, the speed is higher, the thrills are greater, and you could all finish with a faster time.

TEAM TIME TRIALING

Team time trials can be contested by teams ranging from two riders right up to full professional teams of nine riders. There are two ways to ride a team time trial on the road and it can be one of the most spectacular and high-speed events you will ever ride.

1. A two-up time trial will always be ridden with one rider behind the other, each one taking a hard turn on the front while the other rests behind. When the time comes for the leading rider to pull over, he or she moves over to one side and eases off the power for a couple of seconds while the other rider maintains the race pace. The length of each rider's turn depends on what is agreed between the two of them, but normally two-up turns are longer (20 seconds plus) than the faster efforts made on the front of a bigger team, which can be less than 10 seconds each.

2. A bigger team can also ride in a line, like an extended two-up, with the rider on the front swinging off and drifting to the back of the group after his or her turn. It can also be ridden in a double line, more like a hard-working group or breakaway, but with just one rider spearheading the paceline in a constantly revolving stirring pattern.

Knowing when to change over can depend on the terrain, and a good team time trialling outfit will anticipate corners and twisty descents when it can be faster to hold the formation and delay a change-over. On climbs it's more important to stick as closely together as possible, and that means riding at the speed of the slowest climber.

The golden rule of team time trialling is to hold the formation at all costs. Gaps in the group spell disaster – if you cannot hold the wheel in front you need to holler out. For the ultimate exhibition in team harmony watch a team pursuit on the track. The principles of drafting, the art of saving energy by seeking out the calmest pockets of air among groups of riders, albeit at very high speed, are the same.

How to win a road race

There are three ways to cross the line before everyone else.

1. Solo, with the rest either minutes or seconds behind.

2. In a mass sprint from a big group or bunch.

3. Finishing first in a small group sprint.

Tricks of the trade

A cycle race is not the same as a mass-start running event, despite the apparent similarities in format. Thanks quite simply to the advantage to be had from sitting behind another rider, cycling offers the canny cyclist a tempting array of labour-saving ruses which can result in spectacular successes for a weaker rider over stronger rivals. Drafting is what makes cycle racing endlessly fascinating though, for some, frustrating.

If you want to ride hard, in whatever non-solo cycling discipline you choose, you will have to accept that from time to time you will pick up another rider who just sits directly behind you and refuses to take their share of the air-shifting burden. As more and more riders latch onto this cycling conga line, you may feel like a powerful locomotive pulling a string of useless carriages. If you want to lose the hangers on, either to make a breakaway in a road race or just because you would prefer to ride alone in a sportive, you are going to have break the chain. There are numerous ways to do this.

- Make an explosive effort. Timing is everything: try to surprise the others by making your attack at the bottom of a climb, when the drafting effect is rapidly diminishing. Or go from a few riders back so that you are really flying when you pass the first rider in the line.

- Think about taking a shorter line if you are attacking on a corner, but always make sure you are riding safely and head up. Try to create space between you and the others as soon as you can – you do not want to have another rider jumping onto your wheel just as you are flying the nest.

- A surprise element can work wonders – it's no good accelerating with the whole peloton sitting right behind you, possibly sniggering at your futile attempts to ride them off your wheel. A temporary lull, when the group takes a breather over the top of a climb or when they are taking on fuel, is a good moment to spring one on them.

- Be stealthy. Quietly click into a gear in which you can launch the move and wind up to attack speed without changing up. It has to be just right though – too big and you will be labouring at just the point when you need to be punching at the pedals. Too small and you will rev out before hitting top speed. Don't telegraph your move to the others by looking around, throwing your bottle away, or pummelling your chest.

- The most effective attack requires a short near-maximal effort lasting only a handful of seconds. This is followed by no more than a few minutes at your anaerobic threshold while the gap is being established and held or increased. To remain clear of the bunch a high level of effort will be required, similar to riding a time trial.

- It is possible to just ride away from someone sitting on your wheel, despite the big differences in air resistance. You can do it if you are much stronger than the other rider, especially when the road starts to go uphill. Even the gentlest of uphill gradients can be enough to break a weaker follower.

- The fact that you are on the front and prepared to make the pace can put the wheelsuckers under such psychological pressure that they allow you to ride away from them.

- Quite often the reason why one rider follows another and will not come through to share the pacemaking is that he is suffering so much that he simply cannot do so. Even a small change of pace could split the group or result in the strong rider inexorably pulling away. Size up the opposition – if you can see they are hurting badly they might just let you go.

- It's better to save all your energy and ingenuity for one successful attack than to fritter away your reserves on several moves that are chased down or simply fizzle out. Good bike riders are constantly scrutinising the other riders, the terrain and how far there is to go. Making one big attack is something that needs to be planned and executed with as many elements as possible of your ideal scenario in place.

- Be crafty. One or two sham attacks, in which you make 'soft' accelerations which are chased down after a few minutes, can lull your rivals into a false sense of security. When you make your big move, at 100 per cent effort, the bunch may let you go a long way before they realise that you have hoodwinked them.

TIP

Get rid of heavier sprinter types from a breakaway by attacking over the tops of hills.

It's no good being crafty in training, the time to be crafty is in a race.

Barry Hoban, winner of eight stages in the Tour de France and Classics winner

GET USED TO FAST STARTS

One of the hardest things to get used to when riding in a bunch of cyclists, in either a race or a sportive, is fast starts. Whether it is just down to fresh legs and enthusiasm and nerves, or the stronger riders making a quick and immediate cull of the weaker ones, a fast start is something that you need to be primed for.

At the extreme end, a professional cycle race will often kick off with a brutal injection of speed, up to 40mph, inside the first hour. This is generally the time when the first break is being established. As this is a move which can stay away for a long time (gaining valuable exposure for each rider's team sponsors), a lively contest between teams and riders is guaranteed.

In amateur racing the motivation for a fast start has more to do with weeding out the less fit riders, but it also just reflects the thrill of riding in a big group. Fresh legs and big bunches of riders are where the highest speeds can be reached, and you can easily find yourself speeding along at 30mph in close to top gear. Flying along like this can last for several minutes, interspersed with brief periods of little or no effort, then followed by another blast.

Coping with the stresses, changes of pace and nerves of a fast start can be done by:

- Warming up before the start. Include some short sprints, just enough to 'open up' the legs.

- Get psyched. Tell yourself it will be fast and painful, but that the pace will inevitably ease off.

- Don't eat a big piece of cake just before the start as you don't want to feel bloated or uncomfortable. Sip on water or an energy drink and take a caffeine gel instead.

- If you roll out in the second half of the bunch you risk getting caught in the wrong end of a split or stuck behind a crash. Aim to be in the first third if you can. Remember, you all have to go the same speed to keep up and it's much better to 'do unto others' than 'be done unto'!

- You can train for a fast start, with intervals, fartlek intervals and motor-paced training, but there is nothing better than the real thing – the intensity and unpredictability of a mass start is almost impossible to replicate in training.

Road sprinting

Riding away from a big group of cyclists is one of the great endeavours in cycling, but it's also one of the hardest things to do, and can depend on numerous variables falling into place.

It's more likely that you will arrive at the finish with other riders around you. It's at this point, if you want to be first across the line, that you will have to put in a far more explosive effort if you want to lever open a race-winning gap.

It's a situation that every cyclist who rides with others will face from time to time – ranging from a one-on-one sprint to the café stop, to the mass charge to the line on the Champs Elysées to win the final stage of the Tour de France. You may not consider yourself a sprinter, and there is no doubt that some riders are better suited to sprinting than others – but if you do not even acquaint yourself with the basics, your success rate will be substantially reduced.

Every sprint is different, with endless permutations contributing to the outcome. There are some basic elements to consider, however.

- Select a gear that can be wound up to your sprinting speed, with a dozen revs at maximum power pedalled out of the saddle.

- It's better to sprint on a one-tooth smaller gear than one tooth too big, as on the bigger gear you will just get bogged down and changing up the cassette under load will lose precious fractions of a second. If you find you are revving out on a smaller gear the change to a bigger gear is smoother and faster.

- Take advantage of any opportunity to surprise the others, by either going a little earlier than expected or jumping from behind the leading few riders on their blind side.

- If you have teammates who are willing to work for you, follow their wheels as they keep the pace high near the front of the group, and unleash your sprint at the highest speed possible when the last teammate swings off.

- Sprint in a straight line, as efficiently and aerodynamically as possible. Anything you can do to reduce wind resistance at 30mph will save energy.

- If in doubt lead it out. If you find yourself on the front with 250m to go and are not overly confident, a race can be won by kicking as hard as possible and going as fast you can in the manner of a runner kicking for the finish. After a long event a sprint is more a test of reserves and desire than of tactics and genetics.

- If you are not confident of beating stronger sprinters in your group, consider a surprise attack in the final kilometre. You will need to put in a massive effort to gain a gap and then hold it for 30 seconds or so, but this type of move can outwit the sprinters.

Rod Ellingworth has coached the world's best road sprinter, Mark Cavendish, since he was a junior racer. This is his take on why 'Cav' is the best.

'He's naturally fast. When he was a junior he was never the fittest racer, but no matter how much he got hammered in a race he could always sprint at the end of it.

'Over the years we've got him fitter and refined his speed. He's short, so he's already aerodynamic, but he uses techniques that British Cycling's track sprinters like Sir Chris Hoy and Victoria Pendleton use.

'He keeps his head low but looking forward so air flows smoothly over it. He has his arms tucked in and he stays loose so if there is any bumping in the sprint with the other riders he can absorb it and not bounce off them.

'No one can accelerate as quickly as Cav, so he uses that and often goes quite early in a sprint. His lead-out riders take him to 60km/h but then, because he is so quick and light for a sprinter, he can accelerate to 70 and 75km/h quicker than anyone, which gives him a gap.

'But then he backs off a bit, which does two things. It gives him a fraction of recovery and it makes his rivals think they will catch him so they go all out. Then he goes again, and because he is aerodynamic and has less drag acting on him he keeps his speed all the way to the line.

'Most of the work we did was to get Cav fitter and to climb better so that he would get to the end of a race fresh. But I reckon that he probably sprints every time he goes out on his bike.

'Cav likes to train with a group, and like all cyclists they sprint for signposts all the time. But because it's Cav the young ones really try to beat him, which keeps him sharp.

'For the rest he's ridden a lot of track and I pace him on a scooter a lot in training, so Cav is very comfortable tapping away at 50 to 55km/h in the peloton.

'Others who aren't used to that speed might be thinking this is fast, and be riding with their fingers on the brakes in a tightly packed group. That costs them nervous energy but Cav can ride in tight fast groups in his sleep almost, so it doesn't cost him anything.'

Nearly all in the mind

You have done all the training, achieved your optimum weight and perfected your riding position. You are rested and fuelled up. The bike is in the back of the car, polished and lubed. Well done. Now all you have to do is get out there and extract the absolute maximum out of your preparation and talent.

Sounds easy, doesn't it? But the mental part of how you perform on a given day is something that can take years to master, and even at the very highest level of sport it regularly makes the difference between first place and first loser. In fact, take heart because elite athletes are often hard to separate in terms of their preparation and physical talents – they are all pretty much equal, and psychology plays a bigger role in the outcome than it does with less highly trained athletes.

That is not to say that your mental approach is not crucial – just that if you have pre-pared correctly for an event then you are already at a psychological advantage next to those who have fallen short in their own training and wellbeing.

TIP

Once a breakaway is established only do as much work as the rest of the riders in it.

'DON'T FEED YOUR INNER CHIMP'

Steve Peters is British Cycling's sports psychiatrist, and one of the people credited with adding to the enormous and growing success British cyclists have had over the last 10 years.

His job is complex and tailored to each individual athlete and every member of BC's performance cycling section, but one of his key phrases is 'Don't feed your inner chimp'. Basically the inner chimp is the emotional voice in your head. Peters reckons that although emotion might be why you race, it should have no part in the actual process of racing.

'You need to keep everything cold, live in the moment and calmly go through the process of your build-up and once you are in the race everything you do must be based on logic and on doing the right thing at the right time,' he says.

So, you need to be 'at the races' whenever you compete. Focus on what you are doing and not on the result you want because you cannot control that. Just do the best with what you can control, play your cards intelligently and don't make tactical decisions based on ego.

Kit bag checklist

From the start of the season, pack a sports bag with the basics in it all the time and you won't have to run around every weekend packing it afresh. It's worth buying extra inner tubes and even a 'race' helmet which you could leave in the bag, ensuring they never get forgotten.

You will also need to take a track/stirrup pump and a pair of spare wheels if you want to warm up on your training wheels or if you want to use another type of tyre for an off-road event. Spare tyres and even a spare bike could also be worthwhile for cyclo-cross and mountain-biking.

Always take a couple of plastic bags in which to put your dirty or wet clothing and your shoes after the event. If possible, travel to the event in your riding gear, wearing leg warmers or tracksuit bottoms and a warm top and hat. Wear comfortable shoes or sandals, especially in the summer.

For the bike

- Two spare inner tubes and tyre levers
- A spare tyre (hopefully folding)
- Allen keys and basic toolkit
- Mini pump

For you

- Long-sleeve jersey and jacket
- Gilet top
- Rain coat
- Cycling mitts and gloves
- Cotton cap, bandana or helmet liner
- Arm and leg warmers
- Sports sunglasses
- Overshoes – light and heavyweight
- Oversocks
- Helmet and shoes
- Bottles filled with water and energy/recovery drinks
- Your race energy fuel in bottles, gels, bars
- Post-race snack or treat
- Basic first-aid kit
- Embrocation for dry and wet conditions
- High-factor suntan cream
- Safety pins for numbers
- A towel and flannel to clean embrocation off hands and legs
- Warm hat
- Eau de cologne to remove embrocation
- Your racing licence, wallet and mobile phone

Tactics are a bit over-rated. If you are the strongest, tactics don't matter so much.

Johan Bruyneel, ex-pro rider and team manager for Lance Armstrong's seven Tour de France victories.

Three minutes

That's how long, or thereabouts, it takes to get a break established in a road race. You attack, or answer someone else's attack, a couple more get up to you and the break is on. Well, not quite. You now have to get a gap that's too big for all but your best rivals to jump across, and this requires three minutes of absolute eyeballs-out effort.

The initial attack is just that, the start of a breakaway. Now you've got to go hard again. Be committed. Each rider must hammer through to the front to take their turn and really drive. There won't be much time to recover as the others will hammer through too. It will hurt, but three minutes of this will see your break established. Then you can settle down into longer turns, but not as intense, to stay away.

Why three minutes? Because that is about as long as anyone can exercise at their VO_2max, or their maximum oxygen capacity. If you keep going that hard you will have to slow down, a lot. You are working at your maximum, but the rest have to do the same to keep up, which is why the strongest get away in this situation. Once your break is established you'll need to work at around your anaerobic threshold to stay away, and that's time trial pace, which you should be able to keep up for an hour or more.

So three minutes is a very crucial number in road racing and it should help you shape your training. You need to do intense intervals of 30 seconds to three minutes to get as close to your genetic VO_2max as possible. Don't do all your training like that – you need threshold efforts and endurance sessions too. Once every one or two weeks is the way to build VO_2max and racing will help too.

The main thing, though, is to recognise and embrace this three-minute rule. When you have decided that this is the time to make your move, explode in your attack and hammer as if your life depends on it. It's the only way to form a break that will stay away with strong riders, thus increasing the odds of you winning.

RIDER STORY

Barry Hoban is a winner of eight stages in the Tour de France and one of only three British winners of Classics.

'Unless you are the strongest, and I mean strongest by a big margin, you have to be crafty and play your cards right when you race. There are a number of riders in any race who could win it, but not all in the same way. Some will need the hills to get a gap, some will be able to ride hard on the flat, and others will want the race to end in a sprint. My most successful way to win was to outsprint a breakaway group, either a small or a big one.

'The first thing you need to learn is to stay near the front of the bunch so you can attack or react to others attacking. That means being in the first quarter of the field and holding your place there, which as you get more experience will become easier. You also need to recognise when attacks will go, both in terms of the terrain and what is happening in the race.

'For example, if you watch racing on TV, have you noticed that it's often the third attack in a short time that succeeds? What happens is a rider goes and someone bridges, but then more counterattacks from fresh legs bring them back. As soon as that happens some more riders try their luck, but the same thing happens. More fresh legs, different ones this time, bring them back. That's the signal for you to attack, one or two riders might get up to you but that's good.

'But once they do, suddenly there are no fresh legs left in the group. Now you are away, and if you really drill it to get the break out of sight of the others, chances are you'll stay away. Then you can start thinking about getting rid of the others nearer the finish or winning the sprint. Of course that is only one way of doing it, but it is a common one.'

Injury and overtraining

This is not a chapter that will be read with great enthusiasm: after all, who wants to know about the pain and misery of an injury from a crash or physical weakness? You might also believe that overtraining is a condition which only affects riders who spend more time on their bikes than in their beds. It's assumed that only professionals and obsessives who put in 20 or more hours per week are at risk of burning themselves out. Not true.

Cycling is not a risk-free activity. From time to time you will fall off your bike and the resulting bruises, cuts and abrasions will entail at least a few days off. If you are unlucky enough to sustain broken bones in a heavier impact, the length of the lay-off will be in weeks or months. Whatever the damage, the aim must be to recover as quickly as practicable, maintain as much fitness as possible, and resume training at the appropriate intensity.

Coping with a cycling-related injury is one of the things that every experienced rider has been through. In some ways it's one of cycling's boy scout badges – hard on the heels of a roadside puncture repair – and one that's earned and worn with a degree of pride. Overtraining is not the same: this is an invisible impediment to your cycling. You'll get some sympathy if you are covered in plasters and bandages, or have your shoulder in a sling, but the lassitude and fretfulness associated with overtraining can do the opposite. It can even lead to ridicule – tell people that you are overtrained and are taking some time off, and they may choose not to believe you, assuming that you are over-dramatising for the sake of a bit of time off.

But overtraining is a very real hazard for anyone undertaking a structured training programme, even if the weekly workload is less than 10 hours. If you are not a professional rider, a busy lifestyle needs to be carefully managed to ensure that training and resting are a natural and enjoyable part of the working week. And, unlike a physical injury, which in most cases can be recovered from in a given timeframe, overtraining can lay waste to whole seasons and more if it is not recognised and tackled at the earliest opportunity.

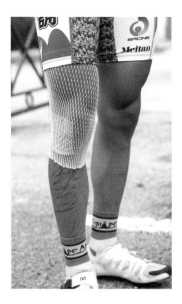

Crash-related injuries

Grazes

'Gravel rash' is the most common type of injury when you slide off a bicycle, sustaining abrasions to the knees, hips, buttocks and elbows. Ask any rider with a few years' experience and they will show you the scars. Bruising is also likely to appear in the same areas and it is the discomfort of riding with both that can require at least a few days off the bike. To protect against gravel rash a pair of track mitts can save your hands, and a base layer under your cycling jersey adds a second defence against abrasion.

Clean up grazes using water diluted with an antiseptic, like Dettol, making sure that all traces of grit are removed. If there are bigger objects in the wound, dress it and get medical help to remove the objects and clean it up. A graze can look very gory and red and might bleed at first. After cleaning the wound, if it continues to weep or bleed, put a plaster or bandage onto it. When it starts to dry out and there are no signs of infection, open the graze up to fresh air as much as possible to speed the healing process. Ensure that your tetanus injections are up to date.

Cuts

Cuts are more serious than gravel rash and require faster and more professional treatment. A cyclist can receive a nasty cut injury in the event of a collision, as opposed to a slide. Apply a dressing and pressure with a bandage and raise the injury above heart level to slow bleeding. A serious cut will need medical attention and possibly stitches so be prepared to make a trip to casualty. If you think you are going to faint, sit down and drink something sweet like cola.

Breaks

A heavy impact can result in a broken bone – most commonly a collarbone, followed by ribs and wrists. You will know about it when you break a bone, it's going to really hurt! There may be swelling too, but whatever the damage it will hurt a lot. All you can do is support the affected area in the most comfortable position, using a sling if possible, and get yourself to a hospital for treatment.

Most breaks will require medical treatment and a lay-off for however long it takes for the bone to heal. Some hand injuries can be treated with a cast, which makes riding possible, if only on a turbo trainer. A broken collarbone can also heal quickly and training can continue if the turbo is set up to allow one-handed riding.

Cracked ribs are as painful as anything but they are not usually treated. Although they can continue to cause stabbing pains when you breathe deeply, riding can continue while the ribs heal. If your rib punctures a lung, though, prepare for a few days in hospital and a lot of painkillers while the medics ensure that your lung does not collapse or you don't pick up an infection.

> **TIP**
>
> Always carry a mobile phone with the battery fully charged.

Head injuries

Even a small bump on the head can lead to a serious brain injury, so if you do hit something and feel at all dizzy, sleepy or cannot remember stuff, you need to get yourself checked out as soon as possible. Do not ride or do strenuous exercise for 24 hours after an incident and try to be around other people who can keep an eye on your behaviour.

One thing that a helmet does very well is protect the head from minor impacts, which could be serious if the rider is bareheaded. For that reason alone it is worth wearing a helmet every time you go out riding. It is just as important to wear a helmet off-road, as in remote areas a crash could leave you totally isolated, so you need to take extra care of your safety. An off-road incident can be far less predictable than a road crash, with rocks, tree stumps and low-hanging branches posing serious hazards to the unwary cyclist.

RICE

An at-home treatment for bumps, bruises and strains, RICE stands for 'Rest Ice Compression Elevation'.

TABLE 11.1: RICE PROCEDURE	
Rest	Stop training for a few days until the pain and stiffness start to recede.
Ice	Place ice on the affected area for 15 minutes every hour on the first evening, then 15 minutes every 2 hours the next day. Use crushed ice or frozen peas in a bag, with a tea towel around it to prevent burning.
Compression	Wear an elasticated bandage over the area to reduce swelling and blood flow.
Elevation	Lift the area if possible, to reduce swelling and blood flow.

Training-related injuries

Cycling is a non-weight-bearing activity and as such its toll on the body is minimal compared to impact or contact sports, like running and football. Correct bike setup is crucial to a pain-free ride. In the event of a riding-related injury, the first port of call must be the bike itself, as it is quite possible that the problem is related to the setup or even a damaged piece of equipment. (For bike setup tips see Chapter 3.)

Knees

Pain in the knees can destroy a season, or worse. Aches and pains in other parts of the body can be endured or treated without interrupting training and racing. But there is no point in riding if you cannot push hard on the pedals. Overuse can be a factor, but more often it is a setup issue that is to blame and a coach or setup expert is the first person to consult. They will look at saddle height, crank length, pedals and shoes, looking for incorrect setup or damage leading to incorrect alignment. Failing that, a physiotherapist or osteopath could diagnose an overuse injury, pain from a non-cycling injury or degeneration.

Typical causes of knee pain are:

- Saddle too high or low
- Saddle set too far forward or back
- Incorrect shoe plate position
- Labouring on big gears
- Damaged components – often a bent pedal
- Pedal and shoe anomalies between bikes and shoes
- Unequal leg length
- Twisted riding position due to another injury
- Pain from non-cycling knee injury
- Hereditary joint pain

Knees and pedals

If the saddle is at the correct height, the most likely culprits of knee pain are the pedals and shoes. Modern clipless pedal systems come with a variety of locking mechanisms with degrees of float adjustment from rigid, or zero float, to free lateral and sideways movement. Shoes come with drillings for various different plates or cleats, and the construction ranges from completely rigid (usually with a carbon sole) to flexible (leisure mountain bike or touring shoe). A rider might have three different pairs of shoes for use with three separate pedal types, each requiring its own shoe plate and range of adjustment.

Just getting all the systems matched up is hard enough, as there can be big differences in shoe plate design, making alignment a headache in the lateral as well as vertical plane. Pedal and shoe choice, foot position and float are all highly personal and correct adjustments can only be arrived at with a fairly cautious approach. If knee pain flares up, changes should only be made in small increments, as the last thing you want to do is exacerbate the problem.

TABLE 11.2: KNEE PAIN

Pain area	Could be	Try this
Front of knee (anterior)	Saddle too low or too far forward	Raise saddle and put it back
	Riding overgeared on hills	Reduce stress on knees pedalling faster in a lower gear
	Cadence too low	Pedal fast on flatter routes
	Cranks too long	Use shorter cranks
Back of knee (posterior)	Saddle too high or too far forward	Lower saddle and put it forward
	Too much float	Reduce float
Inside of knee (medial)	Feet pointing outwards	Adjust cleats to point feet forwards or inwards
	Too much float	Reduce float
	Excessive spring release tension	Soften spring release tension
	Feet too wide apart (Q-factor)	Adjust shoes towards cranks or use narrower cranks
Outside of knee (lateral)	Feet pointing inwards	Adjust cleats to point feet outwards
	Too much float	Reduce float
	Feet too close together (Q-factor)	Adjust shoes away from cranks or spacer between pedal and crank, or use wider cranks

Back

Back pain can be the result of an earlier injury (crash- or exercise-related), incorrect bike setup, weak core strength and flexibility, and incorrect riding technique. Short-term back pain issues can be due to fatigue on long rides over poor road surfaces, often made more uncomfortable when the rider is on a very rigid machine. Unlike knee pain, which can be harder to diagnose, it should be easy to identify back pain and at least begin to treat it.

TABLE 11.3: BACK PAIN	
Back pain	**Correction**
Occurs on long rides	Do shorter rides, work on core strength and flexibility
Too stretched out	Fit a shorter stem, raise the bars and adjust brake levers, improve core strength and flexibility
Riding out of the saddle	Use lower gears and pedal faster, work on core strength
Constant nagging	Check alignment of bike setup, see a physio or an osteopath
Stiff racing equipment	Change bike (carbon can be more forgiving than aluminium) or parts, fit fatter tyres at lower pressures

Contact points

It may be a non-weight-bearing sport but a cyclist still has to sit on the bike, hold the bars and push on the pedals. These five contact areas are particularly susceptible to aches, pains and infections.

Saddle

The saddle area is the one that most non-cyclists worry about and sometimes for good reason. Regular riders should not suffer the discomfort that occasional pedallers experience in the saddle area, as the skin and muscles harden themselves to the pressure from the saddle after a few rides. Wearing cycling shorts with good quality seat pads is essential. Wash them after every ride and keep the seat pad softened with antibacterial cream.

A cyclist should take pride in remaining scrupulously clean in the saddle area – if you don't have a bidet, get used to taking a 'squaddy wash' in the bath before putting your shorts on. Get in the habit of it and use plenty of soap to avoid saddle sores, infections, saddle boils and infected follicles.

An uncomfortable saddle or poor position on the bike can result in a chafing injury, so ensure that you are happy with your saddle choice. If you find that you are moving around in the saddle to the point of chafing, review your setup and riding style. The good news is that a fit, strong cyclist riding at their racing weight pushes harder on the pedals, lifting their bodyweight off the saddle and reducing pressure on the saddle area.

Feet

Cycling is hard on the feet, which have to endure extremes of weather, temperatures high and low and lots of rain. They may not have to withstand the constant impact of running but a cyclist's foot has to push down on a rigid sole many thousands of times in a single ride. Modern cycling shoes can be incredibly stiff, thanks to carbon fibre soles, and finding a pair that suits your foot shape is vital. Shoes with heat-mouldable soles and orthotic inserts are both worth considering for a custom fit.

A foot injury through cycling is rare, but it's very important to select a pair of shoes which do not pinch the sides of the feet and allow some movement for the toes in the front of the shoe. The shape and curvature of the sole is also a personal thing – try several different pairs to find which suits you best.

Go for the lightest, best-ventilated shoes you can afford and when it rains or the temperature drops below 10°C, wear oversocks and thermal or waterproof overshoes. For commuting or winter riding it is also worth buying a pair of mountain bike shoes which are more weatherproof and have a grippy sole for walking.

Hands

Vibration from the bars can make hands go numb and the palms and wrists ache. If you suffer from pain in your hands while cycling try wearing track mitts with thicker palms or gel inserts. You can also double wrap your bars with tape or use a gel tape, which should damp out a fair amount of vibration from the road. Riding position can also play a part – try raising the bars a little or shortening the stem to take some weight off your wrists and hands.

Eyes

Cyclists do not wear sunglasses just for the pose; there are good reasons for protecting the eyes on a bike. Keeping the constant breeze out of the eyes is the main one, especially on descents when the eyes can start streaming and a fly strike could have lethal consequences. Good quality shades will also reduce glare and enhance vision in bright sunlight. In the summer, sunglasses can protect against dust and hay fever, preventing infections like conjunctivitis. If you don't like wearing glasses, wash your eyes with water after or during long summer rides.

Skin

The increasing risk of skin cancer makes it absolutely essential that you apply high factor (above 20) sunscreen whenever riding in strong direct sunlight. Sports-specific sunscreens, available in various dispensers, can be very high factor, long-lasting and resistant to water and sweat. Apply to face, arms and legs as well as the back of the neck.

Overtraining

There are many symptoms of overtraining and you need to be able to recognise them to take action, fast. Overtraining occurs when you lose the balance between training, rest and real life. You might think that only a professional rider, putting in over 20 hours a week on the bike, can become overtrained. Hours on the bike alone are rarely the reason for overtraining.

A professional rider can handle large doses of training and intensity because they recover from each session with adequate rest periods, often aided by massage and increasingly sophisticated nutrition and recovery strategies. By scientifically monitoring their training programme, a pro rider can also detect the symptoms of overtraining at the earliest opportunity and tweak the schedule accordingly.

There is lots to learn from how a top rider handles the stresses of training but one thing that most of us cannot ignore, nor would we want to, is a full and busy life outside cycling. Don't forget that a pro rider's job is to train, race and rest. And that's about it. The reality is that you can become overtrained on less than 10 hours' training a week. That might be because your body is not handling a high-intensity training programme, or it might be that your non-cycling commitments are preventing you from resting your body and mind.

A training programme that does not suit you, or is not periodised, can result in overtraining. It could be that the amount of high-intensity sessions are just too hard for you at that point in your training cycle, or that you are physiologically not suited to a certain programme. Add the individual circumstances of your home and work life and you can see why there can never be a prescription for training burnout.

Put simply, overtraining occurs when the workload results in breakdown (catabolism) rather than build-up (anabolism). Your performance on the bike stalls and can even go into decline. The symptoms vary, from a constant feeling of fatigue and listlessness, to health, weight and mental problems. Here are some of the symptoms.

Drop in performance
This occurs when you are unable to lift your performance to the highest level during hard training, riding and racing. Also, an inability to push the heart rate to maximum becomes apparent.

Fatigue and loss of performance
More than just the tiredness experienced after a long or hard training session, a constant feeling of lethargy and fatigue can be a sure sign of overload. It will also manifest itself on the bike. A mistake that many cyclists make at this point is to push harder, thereby digging themselves into an even deeper hole. It's natural to have an occasional off-day on the bike – an experienced rider will recognise this and have the confidence to batter their way through it in the knowledge that they are not overtraining.

Elevated resting heart rate
Get into the habit of taking your resting heart rate, in the morning after waking. If your heart rate is 10 per cent above its normal resting rate, you may not have recovered from a session. Try to replicate the same conditions every morning: wake up and lie in bed to take your heart rate.

Insomnia
If you are not getting eight hours' quality sleep each night then you need to tailor your programme accordingly. Sustained periods of disrupted sleep can indicate overtraining.

Niggling coughs and colds
Burnout can suppress the immune system, leading to colds and upper respiratory infections. Minor injuries can also take longer to heal. In women, overtraining can lead to a loss of menstrual periods (amenorrhoea).

Stiffness and soreness
Normal riding on a correctly set up machine should not result in muscular pain or stiffness. If soreness persists for more than 48 hours it can be a sign that you are not recovering from hard training.

Weight loss
If you are losing weight over a period of weeks, without consciously reducing your calories and with any of the other symptoms listed here, the body could be struggling to cope with the workload imposed upon it.

Mental state
One of the most reliable signals of overtraining, changes in your mental state may well be identified by your partner or workmates before yourself. Feeling angry,

irritable, depressed or apathetic are all signs that you may not be handling your training programme. Compare your feelings with other times when you were super-enthusiastic and could not wait to get out for a ride. If you are feeling negative and demotivated you need to recharge the batteries.

Avoid overtraining

While periodisation of training might not be as fashionable as it used to be, one of the standout benefits of a training programme composed of medium-term blocks of varying loads is the opportunity to allow the body to avoid overtraining. Taking into account all other factors, it's your training programme which ultimately governs whether or not you are likely to overtrain.

A well-planned programme will have periods of rest and recovery factored in, often during the heaviest chunks of training when enthusiasm can be high but the risk of tipping the balance is also ever-present. It can feel wrong to take your foot off the gas during an intensive build-up phase, but the results will be worth it.

If you feel the effects of overtraining coming on before your training programme has allowed for it, then you need to alter the programme and back off before it's too late. Be prepared to modify the training plan by adding rest days or reducing the intensity.

If you are coming back from a lay-off due to injury or illness it is even more important to reverse-taper your return to riding, building back up with progressively longer rides with plenty of recovery and a sound nutrition and hydration strategy. It is a myth that overtraining only occurs after many months of riding – just ten days' riding without a proper base can result in the signs of burnout.

Recovering from overtraining

First you need to be sure that you are overtrained, especially if the symptoms are fatigue- or illness-based. A medical check-up, maybe a blood test, will determine whether you are suffering from a condition unrelated to cycling.

If the burnout is due to overtraining, the only cure is rest. Take at least 10 days to two weeks off and try to get as much quality sleep, nutrition and hydration as possible. Let your body recover and de-stress your head if you can by changing your routine and having some fun. A holiday springs to mind. When you start riding again take it easy and keep it that way for another 10 days.

Review your training and modify your programme, especially the amount of interval sessions and high-intensity riding. Add rest days. If you are racing or riding hard over big mileages on a weekly basis, consider dropping some events in favour of targets spread further apart.

Use your training diary to record your daily heart rate, weight and hours of sleep. The more information you have in your diary, the easier it will be to spot a trend that points to overtraining. Try to identify patterns of behaviour at work and home that also lead to the stress that you experienced before burnout occurred.

FOCUS ON

The psychological aspects of injury

Your mind is a powerful force in helping your body recover. An injury or illness is difficult for anyone to cope with: it gets in the way of plans and can cause all sorts of problems. For an athlete it can be especially difficult, but adopting a positive frame of mind really helps. Here is a strategy, split into straightforward stages, that will help you do just that.

- *Accept:* The first step to recovery is accepting what has happened. The best way to do this is to reframe an injury's significance by thinking of it as the only thing you have no influence over. However, treatment, rehab and recovery are up to you, so focus on them instead.

- *Own it:* This is your injury – find out everything you can about it and how to treat it. Get involved with the process of treating it.

- *Don't get isolated:* Keep going to races or meeting your cycling friends in some other way. They will sympathise and encourage. And they will be quick to stop you taking your situation too seriously, too.

- *Use some tools:* Goal setting, self talk, imagery and visualisation have all been shown to help recovery from injury. There are plenty of books on how to use these tools.

- *Be positive:* You will come back if you follow some logical predetermined steps to recovery. It's like climbing a hill – if you are still moving, no matter how slowly, you will get to the top.

PLANNING THE RECOVERY

· *Agree a plan:* Most likely this will be with your physiotherapist. Ask them to break your rehabilitation into measurable stages. Make suggestions, don't just listen and nod.

· *Stick to it:* A plan is no good if you don't follow it. Be patient, but if you are progressing quickly, seek advice and revise the process.

· *Eat well:* You need good food to help heal the injury and to fuel the rebuilding process. If you feel you are putting on weight cut down on carbs, but not protein. Eat a wide range of vitamin- and mineral-rich foods. Good fats, like those from oily fish, will help to reduce inflammation naturally.

· *Use common sense:* Making a comeback after overtraining can be an emotional and nerve-wracking time, as each training ride could signal a new surge of energy, or a worrying feeling of the overtraining symptoms from before. You need to be coldly analytical about your schedule, prepared to change it if necessary and accept setbacks by working out ways to overcome them.

LANCE ARMSTRONG'S LOGICAL APPROACH

Lance Armstrong's comeback in 2009 was surrounded by hype, but he's stuck rigidly to an intelligent plan. He did tests before he announced his comeback to see if he was still ballpark for a pro rider. He put in a series of base-training periods, with little peaks for more tests. He had a problem with upper-body muscle, which he did specific training to reduce. He broke his collarbone, which was a setback, but he sought out the best experts at every stage of his treatment. After racing the Tour of Italy in a really controlled manner, he began to work on a peak for the Tour de France. Armstrong is coldly logical and is never goaded into a fight he cannot win. Logic, not emotion, governs a successful comeback. If the worst does happen, then let it govern yours.

RIDER STORY

Ben Greenwood is a top British road racer with the Rapha-Condor team.

Greenwood's injury wasn't a traumatic break, or anything that came on all of a sudden, but it was due to a muscular imbalance that affected his knee. The strange thing about his case was that he knew nothing of it until an operation on his wisdom teeth caused him to have some time off his bike.

'After the operation I was advised to have a week off training and do nothing. I did that, I just sat around and read some books. Then I started back by doing an easy ride, but during the ride my right knee began popping. Next day was our team presentation in London, but I could hardly walk and by night the knee even hurt while I was sitting still.

'I went straight home and booked an appointment with one of British Cycling's team doctors and he diagnosed the problem as a maltracking patella, which meant that my right kneecap wasn't moving in the groove where it should fit.

'The doctor said that it was caused by a combination of a tight iliotibial (IT) band and weak gluteal muscles, and referred me for physio at the English Institute of Sport. The physio who worked on me there reckoned that I'd had the underlying problem for years, but the knee pain had started because I'd sat around a lot during the week I had off after my operation.

'Apparently sitting causes extra tightness and that allowed the underlying muscular imbalance to take over. When I started riding again it pulled my knee out of track. He said that the imbalance had been a time bomb waiting to go off and it would have caused the problem eventually.

'The imbalance had to be corrected, and it was a long process, but it gave me time to think about how the problem occurred in the first place. I started to think about how I'd been pedalling. I'd always known that my knees came right across the top tube when I was pedalling. It was like every time each leg went up and down, the knee also went in and out. The physio told me that the weak gluteals caused a lack of stability in my legs, and that in turn caused the tight IT bands.

'I needed to build up my gluteals and other hip muscles to provide a more solid base for my legs to pedal against. I also needed to relieve the tightness in my IT bands, but doing that was really painful.

'To stretch the bands the physio gave me a roller, a cylindrical piece of foam rubber, and I had to lie on my side with the roller under the IT band and drag myself backwards and forwards over it. The first time I did it, it was so painful that I could only do it once.

'I kept at it though, and eventually the IT bands began to stretch. At the same time I did some very specific exercises to strengthen my gluteal muscles. No weights, they were all exercises that used body weight and targeted my hip and gluteal muscles only.

'Once I got the exercise programme going I started riding my bike, but only in a very low gear, and I concentrated all the time on keeping my knee straight. Eventually I built up the miles, the pain got less and only then did I start using bigger gears and making hard efforts. After a while I was able to get back into Premier Calendar races and pick up my racing almost where I'd left off.'

So much to do…

Not so long ago the only way to go out and really test yourself on a bicycle was in an officially sanctioned race. Getting into shape, perfecting your style, fettling your machine and taking care of your diet and health were aspects of bike riding that were associated with a minority of cyclists concerned only with crossing the line first and personal best times.

In English-speaking countries cycling has never been a majority pastime, and racing was something of a cult even among enthusiasts. Knowledge and training advice was passed down at cycling clubs, usually in musty village halls where callow youths would take instruction from their tea-drinking club elders.

Books on training were rare, bought at a young age, pored over and either followed to the letter, or left on the shelf when contradicted by more colourful myths and legends handed down from club mates. After a winter of long training runs, in all weathers on heavy bikes and tyres, the first race of the season would start with a lonely effort against the watch – an early season time trial which stunned the legs and lungs into action.

How much more fun it would have been to have the range of races, challenge events and more varied training rides that today's cyclist can choose from. Cycling has become a mainstream sport in recent times and its widespread benefits for fitness and good health are reflected in the many books, newspaper and magazine articles, and TV programmes that promote cycling. And it's not just training that has undergone a revolution – the amount of tempting challenges for the keen bike rider means there is something for everyone.

Racing remains the pinnacle of achievement for any cyclist and there are many different disciplines, on- and off-road, age group categories and distances that you could consider if you wanted to test yourself against your peers. Don't be put off by licences and rules – they are far less onerous than they appear and if you race locally, your costs can be kept to a minimum.

If you thirst for a challenge but prefer to test yourself against the terrain, then sportive rides offer the best of both worlds. Without a doubt sportives are the success story of modern cycling and they continue to grow in terms of popularity and global spread. If you sometimes wonder how to put all your hard work to good use, this section is designed to plant the seeds of discovery, to inspire you to try something new or travel further afield to experience some epic cycling challenges.

Racing

If there is one thing guaranteed to motivate you to follow a training schedule and live the life of a dedicated athlete, it's the prospect of racing. Through the long winter months when the idea of spending hours in the saddle taking a battering from the cold and rain does not appeal, what better spur can there be than the dream of crossing the line, arms aloft for your first win?

Even if you just want to experience the thrill of riding along in a bunch of cyclists, or feel the life-affirming buzz of nerves as you jostle for position on the start line, racing can give you a cycling high like no other. Winning can be the dream, but it need not be the sole objective – far from it. Racing will improve you as a cyclist in every area, from your physical condition and ability to suffer, to how to pack a kit bag and organise your race day.

You can race two or three times a week, every week through the season, or you can select a few events throughout the year and use them as motivational stepping stones, with non-competitive training and sportive riding in between. The great thing about cycle racing is that there are races from January through to December. There is something for everyone and cycling welcomes new riders, with events for novices, children and older riders.

Racing will change you as a cyclist. Do a few races and you will understand why bikes were made to go fast, to carry you to terrific highs and big lows, and to allow you to live in the moment like nothing else.

Road race

Mass-start road racing is the epitome of cycle racing and the most common form of organised event worldwide. It's also the simplest form of bike racing, setting everyone off together in a bunch and, after a set distance, recording the finishing order of each rider, first to last. Professional road racing on the continent of Europe is built upon one-day road races and multiple days of stage racing from two days to three weeks.

At grass-roots level there are local road racing events taking place every week from March to October, and sometimes through the winter on closed circuits. You can race a one-hour criterium on a short circuit, either on the open road or on a purpose built traffic-free tarmac circuit. On the open road, races for amateurs can go from 80km to around 150km. A pro race will normally be around 200km.

A race is so different to what we experience in our everyday lives. It's all out there in a race, pure competition, and that is a bond all those who take part share.

Allan Peiper

At senior level, racing is by category or age-related, with a points system based on previous results used to classify each category. Age-related racing caters for school-children and for veteran riders over 40, but sometimes under. Women can race in their own category events or often against men or veterans in mixed fields of similar ability. A racing licence will last a year and cover you for third-party insurance as well as affording you the benefits of being a member of a national cycling organisation. Entry fees for each race, often taken on the day, are the only other direct cost.

Time trial
Riding as fast as you can along a measured course remains the purest form of cycle racing for many riders. Always popular in the UK, where there is a long tradition of racing against the clock over fixed distances from 10 to 100 miles, time trialling can be a great way to get into grass-roots racing.

Many clubs still hold evening time trials during the season, which can be entered on the night for the price of a pint of beer. There may only be a dozen riders but you'll get to wear a number on your back and the chance to go as hard as you can over a set course, most often 10 miles out and back or around a circuit.

Stepping up a level, there are events every weekend open to all comers and which must be entered and paid for in advance on a standard form. Typically distances are 10, 25, 50 and 100 miles, and for the ultra-endurance fans, 12 and 24 hours. Any type of bike can be ridden, although to be competitive a road bike with tri-bars or a low-profile TT machine is de rigueur. No matter your machine, however, the beauty of time trialling is that you can test yourself over a measured distance and try to better your time, average speed or training partner!

Time trialling may not be as glamorous and exciting as road racing, but don't let that put you off a branch of the sport that appeals on many levels and is still regarded in professional circles as the ultimate test of a bike rider's strength and concentration. Not for nothing is it called 'the race of truth'.

Cross-country

There's nothing like getting away from it all in the heart of the countryside, away from traffic, on tracks which test your bike handling skills as much as your fitness. Some of the most fun to be had on a bike can be off-road, where you can get closer to nature than on the road, enjoying the sights, sounds and solitude of pedalling on the dirt. Mountain bike racing, or cross-country, is a more intense way to commune with nature. It's a lot of fun and one of the best all-round tests of fitness and bike handling.

In many regions cross-country is not as established or commonplace as the road disciplines, and you will have to be prepared to travel if you wish to compete regularly. This is partly down to the availability of suitable courses – you don't have to have a mountain for a mountain bike race but it helps to have a relatively large circuit with a variety of challenges, climbs, technical descents and so on.

Downhill mountain biking has also stunted the growth of cross-country, diverting many mountain bikers into the thrilling but unathletic pursuit of posting the fastest times on a purely downhill course. Downhill has become so popular that a whole new breed of machine has evolved, with near-motorcycle levels of suspension front and rear, bomb-proof chassis, low saddle height and extra kilos aplenty, making cross-country riding unnecessarily irksome.

If you have a standard mountain bike, with a conventional suspension fork, or dual suspension, there are cross-country races ranging from a short one-hour blast to increasingly popular marathon team events lasting up to 24 hours. There is a more relaxed atmosphere at off-road events, and mountain bike cross-country is a great way to enjoy racing with a little less of the stress and nerves associated with road racing. That is partly down to the people involved but mainly because, although competitors start off in a big bunch, within minutes everyone is spread out and racing pretty much in their own world.

Cyclo-cross

Held on a short circuit and usually lasting one hour plus one lap, cyclo-cross is the best winter workout you can get, and if you can learn to love washing the mud off your bike on a dark wet Sunday afternoon, cross is an absolute blast.

Increasingly popular thanks to its car-free courses and the quality of workout and technical challenges, cyclo-cross is a winter sport running from September to February. It's the perfect off-season antidote to long training rides and a great way to maintain power and top-end fitness. For serious cyclo-cross racers the cross season is the most important half of the year and European-based cross riders can race at least every weekend.

In contrast to a mountain bike cross-country course, which can be set in pretty wild locations, cyclo-cross generally takes place in a parkland setting with lots of fast ride-able sections broken up by technical woods-riding and a small amount of running up steep banks and over obstacles. This encourages racing in a series of short bursts of power, with equally short periods of low-level effort either going downhill or around tricky obstacles.

You can ride a cross race on a mountain bike but most competitors use what looks like a road race bike shod with knobbly tyres. Look a little closer, however, and there are a small number of significant differences – such as cantilever brakes, rerouted cables and larger clearances all round – which make a cross bike uniquely suited to its job of going as fast as possible on the mud. It's main advantage over a mountain bike is its lower weight and larger frame which allows it to be slung over one shoulder when you have to get off and run.

Track
If you live near a banked cycling track then you are a very lucky person. Tracks are few and far between and a covered track with wooden boards even more rare, so if you get the opportunity to ride regularly, get yourself a track bike and enter the wonderful world of fixed wheels, banking and no brakes!

Even if you just use a track for training, either in a group session or simply on your own, the benefits of riding a track bike will pay off handsomely in whatever other cycling disciplines you take part in. If you get the chance to race then you will experience the purest form of cycle sport. Track racing on an indoor track takes place throughout the year, but on an open track, made from either wood or cement, you will be restricted to racing on dry days throughout the racing season. Training might take place on open tracks through the winter, though, so you get to use your track bike all year.

There are many different types of track race to take part in. They can be roughly divided into sprint and endurance events, with the match sprint at one end and a distance event like the scratch race at the other. Just like on the road, there is something for everyone on the track – for stockier, powerful riders mostly suited to the sprint events and for lighter trackies inclined towards the longer distance races. Races can be very short: a time trial can be run in as little as 60 seconds or could last 20 minutes or so. A track programme of events in a typical meeting will have numerous events and there is nothing to stop you from racing in both sprint and endurance races.

Sportive

A sportive is not strictly speaking a race, but it presents a racing-style challenge to riders looking to finish with a high placing, based on their individual ride time.

Inspired by the European 'cyclo-sportif' or 'gran fondo', a sportive or cyclo-sportive is a mass participation ride around a set route, with a finishing time awarded to each rider who completes the route. Sounds like a road race? Well, at the front of a sportive, which might have many thousands of entrants, the event is ridden as seriously as a road race and to finish with the fastest time or inside the top 10 per cent is an achievement to be proud of.

For the majority of riders a sportive is a challenge ride which can be ridden at any level, either full-on with the intention of posting the best time possible, or at a more sociable pace with a like-minded group of riders out to enjoy a scenic ride in the countryside. Terrain plays a major part in the nature of the challenge – hilly routes are often favoured, with lots of climbing to break up the field and to ensure that everyone gets a good workout and, energy permitting, enjoys some lovely views!

COMPLETING THE DISTANCE

For many the biggest challenge of a sportive is not in trying to beat the riders around them, but in completing the distance, which can be from 20 to 100 miles or more. Often there is a choice of rides:

- A short family ride of 20 miles (or 30km) or so

- A half-day ride of about 60 miles (or 100km)

- An all-day event of up to 120 miles (or 200km)

There is a well-established calendar of sportives in Europe, with numerous famous events taking place on the same routes each year and attracting sell-out fields. The most popular of these events take place in the great mountain ranges of Europe, most notably the French and Italian Alps, the French and Spanish Pyrenees and the Italian Dolomites. Climbs include the legendary passes used in the Grand Tours of France, Italy and Spain, and the biggest events take place on closed roads, giving entrants the opportunity to experience the equivalent of a mountain stage as ridden by the pros in one of the tours.

A ride in just one of these tough events, if you are travelling from further afield, incurs overnight costs and demands planning, time and lots of training. It can be quite an achievement and it is certainly no disgrace to do just one a year.

Not quite on the same scale as in Europe, the UK sportive scene is catching up fast, having become popular in a big way in recent years. There is now at least one event every weekend throughout the year, with only a short break in the winter months and, while some sportives are local rides with only a hundred or so riders, there are already some 'classics' with big fields of several thousand entrants. They do not take place on closed roads but are expertly marshalled, with fuel stops and medical and mechanical support just like their continental cousins. Sportives are the fastest-growing branch of cycling and are an ideal way for young and old to test themselves on a big ride.

Touring

Racing, competition, pushing yourself on every ride, processing numbers on the laptop – it can get to you after a while and, before you know it, the cycling palate has become jaded. Putting the fun back into your riding (that's why you got hooked in the first place, right?) is the equivalent of resting with bells on – its mental and physical benefits are an essential reminder of the simple pleasures of cycling.

Maybe, like many keen cyclists, you started out riding fast and have not slowed down since. Taking your time, getting used to the extra weight of luggage and stopping to look at the view might feel strange at first, but the charms of touring will grow on you, and that's a guarantee.

There are no rules for cycle touring; you can disappear for months on end, with your machine loaded with tent and cooking gear, or you can travel light in the company of a couple of mates on an out-and-back one-nighter. For a short tour of a few nights or so, it is not necessary to carry much luggage at all – you could get away with a T-shirt, underwear and a toothbrush if you cycle in baggy shorts and mountain bike shoes.

There are numerous ways to carry a small amount of luggage, ranging from an over-size saddle pack to a saddle bag, rack-mounted bag and side-mounted panniers. Even a small rucksack can be used to carry some gear, but it's much better to let the bike take the strain. Many sports bikes will have mounting points for a rack, which can be fitted in minutes, and mudguards are also worthwhile if you like to sit down in a café with a dry behind!

Don't underestimate the benefits of a touring holiday for your fitness. Several long days in the saddle at a moderate pace can do no harm in the build-up to a season. Base miles are great for endurance and there's plenty to be said for living with the bike for a few days now and then. If you throw in a competitive element, riding hard up the climbs or in team formation for the final hour each day, a tour can be as beneficial as a training camp. And at the end of a long day in the saddle you will surely have earned yourself a hearty meal and a pint of foaming ale, with light banter among friends to add a glow to your cheeks.

Training camp

If you can spare the time – usually a week – and have the funds, a pre-season training holiday is a great way to boost your fitness, preferably somewhere warm and cycling-friendly. Like a touring holiday, a training camp gives you the chance to spend all day on your bike and spend quality time with cycling friends new and old. Above all, it can be a fast track to a higher fitness level before the season has started or during the season itself.

Popular winter and spring training camps for Europeans involve short flights to Spain, where the mountain roads of the southern mainland and the island of Mallorca have long welcomed groups of racing cyclists. Italy and the south of France are also well suited to riding in groups on relatively traffic-free roads. Each camp is different but there is usually at least two ride options each day, with the longer ride lasting at least four hours and a stop. Good roads, warm weather and large bunches of riders guarantee higher than average speeds, and for northerners, more used to 'heavy' roads and even heavier weather, these training rides are a joy.

Training camps should come with a big warning sign, though, as they can result in overtraining and illness, which can negate all the hard-training benefits and even hobble your season. It is easy to get carried away and do too much, resulting in deep fatigue by the middle of the week and complete overload by the end of it. It is essential to arrive at a training camp with a level of fitness that allows you to ride comfortably throughout the week. It is also recommended to take one day very easy during the week, to let some recovery kick in before it's too late. Approached properly, the chance to live like a pro for a week can be a truly memorable experience with results to match when you get home.

FOCUS ON

What excites you

If your desire to do something in cycling doesn't give you goose bumps when you think about it, then maybe it isn't for you. Once you've tried some different forms of racing, or challenges on your bike, you should have a good idea about which kind of cycling you enjoy the most. That's when to specialise, to really go for it. It might be that you like every aspect of racing, which is great, but if you want to excel you nearly always have to pick one thing and go for it.

That doesn't mean you can't ride lots of different kinds of race. Indeed, the best endurance track riders do a lot of racing to build their stamina. Top cyclo-cross riders race on the road for the same reason. Road racers can benefit from some track racing to add a bit of zip and speed to their legs and make them feel comfortable in a high-speed close-spaced group. They sometimes ride cyclo-cross for a good winter workout and to improve their bike handling and reflexes. About the only branch of cycling where the racers don't do much in the way of other events is at the very top end of track sprinting.

The question is, how do you choose which event to specialise in? To a certain extent your genes choose for you. Once you've been cycling for a while you get a feel for what type of cyclist you are. If you win lots of sprints maybe the track is where to go. On the other hand, light, agile and fast riders make good cyclo-cross racers. Got the same thing but with bags of stamina? Then you could be on your way to mountain bike cross-country glory. If you are strong and can go the distance then time trialling might be your thing.

But all of that is logic: there is, however, another test. Think about the racing you have done and think about the racing you enjoy watching on TV. Now, what thrills you? What do you wish you could see yourself doing? What gives you goose bumps? That is the test Bradley Wiggins gave himself when he committed to changing from being one of the best track pursuiters the world has ever seen, into a Tour de France contender. He admits that it was the Tour and road racing that always gave him goose bumps, and that desire was his inspiration.

RIDER STORY

Cadel Evans, 2009 Professional World Road Race Champion and Tour de France podium finisher, was a top mountain biker, twice winner of the World Cup, before he switched to the road.

'Even when I was a mountain biker I wanted to go full time on the road. I just got into mountain biking first and when I began to progress I had to see it through. Road racing appealed to me more.

'Mountain biking is a solo event and I was always more interested in the team dynamic of road racing. I like being part of a team rather than on my own, that's my nature. I also like the feel of history that road racing has, I love reading about the exploits of the riders in the big races all those years ago. What they faced and overcame is amazing. I guess that is what road racing is about, history, tradition and teamwork. All things that I respect.'

Index

w

y